Wit and Wisdom of the Saints

A Year of Saintly Humor

Victoria Hébert and Judy Bauer

Liguori

LIGUORI, MISSOURI

Imprimi Potest:
Richard Thibodeau, C.Ss.R.
Provincial, Denver Province
The Redemptorists

Published by Liguori Publications
Liguori, Missouri
www.liguori.org
www.catholicbooksonline.com

Library of Congress Cataloging-in-Publication Data

Hébert, Victoria.
    Wit and wisdom of the saints : a year of saintly humor / Victoria Hébert and Judy Bauer.—1st ed.
        p. cm.
    Includes bibliographical references and index.
    ISBN 0-7648-0786-2 (pbk.)
    1. Christian saints—Humor. I. Bauer, Judy, 1941– II. Title.

BX4661 .H43 2002
270'.092'2—dc21   2001050508

Printed in the United States of America
06 05 04 03 02   5 4 3 2 1
First edition

DEDICATION

~

To my family
—Denis, Carinne and Mathieu Hébert—
who have, as always, chipped in to make meals,
taken care of the details of life, assisted me in
research, as well as loved me to the max in order
to see this book to its finish. To say I love you all
for it wouldn't be enough!

~

To my mother Margaret Bauer
who put up with "all those books." Thanks!

CONTENTS

~

INTRODUCTION

~

WHY WRITE ANOTHER BOOK on the saints? And at that, a book about their seemingly lighter moments? Isn't that somewhat *taboo*? These were the comments we met with when we had the original idea for this book.

Over the years, in the course of both of our "regular" jobs, we have come across many other books about the saints—and when I say many, I mean reams and reams. Generally speaking, each of these books, to date, gives us a biographical picture of a saint depicting each one as a person who was serious, very pious and, in a great many cases, willing to die for the faith. But when we dug a little deeper, we also saw some of these saints from a different perspective, a more lighthearted one. Even Saint Francis de Sales expressed his concern that hagiographers were depicting saints in an unrealistic manner, citing only their virtues and not the totality of the person. He is quoted as saying: "No harm can be done when we show their lighter sides." Continuing, he stated that writers were even performing a *disservice* to the readers by not showing a complete picture. So, as we took that second, longer and deeper look, like the precious jewels they are, the saints, themselves, revealed more facets of their lives to us—they were witty, they laughed and even made jokes, and some taught using humor. So much more came to light. We began to chuckle, and nod, even uttering an "aha" from time to time. This surprised us, although perhaps it shouldn't have. We asked ourselves: Is it acceptable (or even permissible) to laugh with a person who was martyred? Is humor reserved just for those of us who are not yet saints? Are saints solely serious beings? Why haven't we seen this before—is there something wrong with thinking that saints are joyful people with a sense of humor, or maybe even witty? Is it wrong to look at the unusual, even comical, events in their lives? Should we just look away, ignore the human characteristics we see there?

The idea for this book fits perfectly into what we personally perceive about saints—they are ordinary people who have been "given" extraordinary gifts by Our Lord. In writing this book, we both have come to affirm our belief that these special people, these saints, are so very much like us. Being like us, some were witty and humorous, and others were also dour and, yes, boring. But through their wit and humor, we can certainly identify more closely with them. When we see ourselves to be more like these saints, we will also come to the realization, first, that we, too, could become saints. We all have been granted extraordinary talents— we have a variety of vocations—just like the "officially sainted." All of our vocations are important to Our Lord, given to us out of his love, to be used for his glory.

Perhaps if we show you the wit and wisdom of the saints, you will come to see, as we have, that you, too, have the potential to do great "saintly" things, or maybe you are already doing them.

In all, we see this book as an introduction to the saints, a means for you to see their humanity and their "humanness." And, in the process, if we do happen to bring you a chuckle or an "aha," all the better.

The book itself is divided into twelve chapters, one for each month of the year. The passages about a particular saint that are included in the book are done so according to their feast days. For example, you'll find passages for Saint Francis of Assisi in October (Chapter 10) because his feast day is October 4. And, for a quick and handy reference, there is an alphabetical index included at the end of the book—a quick way to look up your own favorites.

January

~

Fulgentius of Ruspe
(d. 533)

BORN OF NOBLE PARENTS *in Carthage, Fulgentius became a monk over his mother's objections. He was made bishop of Ruspe but was banished to Italy by King Thrasimund, who belonged to the heretical Arians. After the king died in 523, Fulgentius returned home to Ruspe where he edified the people by his example and his persuasive preaching.*

~

Fulgentius endured his final illness calmly and could be heard to pray often: "Lord, grant me patience now, and hereafter mercy and pardon." His doctors prescribed baths as a cure for his illness, but Fulgentius replied pointedly: "Can baths make a mortal man escape his death, where his life has reached its term?"

When miracles were attributed to him, Fulgentius would reply: "A person may be endowed with the gift of miracles and yet may lose his soul."

Basil the Great

(d. 379)

BASIL, ONE OF THE FOUR GREAT DOCTORS of the Western Church, was born in Cappadocia into a deeply Christian family. After studies at Constantinople and Athens, Basil visited various monastic colonies and then founded his own, for which he wrote his rule, which is still followed by monasteries of the East. In 370, he was made metropolitan of Caesarea and took up the fight against heresies. For this purpose, he wrote important theological works.

~

In a letter to his friend Saint Gregory of Nyssa, Basil wryly describes his difficulties with his monastic life on the river Iris: "I blush to tell you what I myself do night and day in my retreat. For I have renounced city occupations, as the occasions of my innumerable misfortunes. But I have not been able to detach myself from myself. I am like those who, on the sea, because they are unaccustomed to sailing, are seasick: they grumble that it is the lifeboat or dinghy, but everywhere they are ill at ease and feel equally sick, for their own bile and their own nausea has followed them. That's about what has happened to us here: we brought our own domestic troubles with us, and are subject to the same troubles everywhere, to such an extent that we have not profited much from our isolation."

Shortly after Basil had become metropolitan of Caesarea, a famine occurred, and Basil spoke strong words against black marketeers: "What will you say to God when he asks you why you dressed the walls of your house, and not your brother, you who hoard your wheat and do not feed the hungry? Whom have I wronged, you ask, by keeping what is my own?...Why do you think [these goods] were for your personal use? It's just as if someone in the theater, having taken a seat, prevented others from entering and making use of what belongs to all. Such is the attitude of those who possess: because they were the first to occupy common property, they think they can appropriate it."

Basil has this to say about the envious: Envy is a gnawing pain which springs from the success and prosperity of another; and this is the reason why the envious are never exempt from trouble and vexation. If an abundant harvest fills the granaries of a neighbor, if success crowns his efforts, the envious man is chagrined and sad. If one man can boast of prudence, talent, and eloquence; if another is rich, and is very liberal to the poor, if good works are praised by all around, the envious man is shocked and grieved.

Basil points out: "Prudence must precede all our actions since, if prudence is lacking, there is nothing, however good it may seem, that is not turned into evil."

JANUARY 3

Genevieve
(d. 500)

PATRON SAINT OF PARIS, Genevieve persuaded inhabitants of that city to remain in Paris rather than flee from the approaching attack of Attila the Hun. She reasoned that other places where people would seek refuge were just as likely to be devastated. Attila abandoned his march toward Paris and was beaten in battle by the Franks. When the Franks also besieged Paris, Genevieve led a fleet out to find food and prevent Parisians from dying of hunger.

~

Genevieve was once heard to scold God in these words: "Well, my God, is this the reward promised by you to those who love and serve you? What has your humble servant done to merit such a severe a punishment?"

JANUARY 5

John Nepomucene Neumann
(d. 1860)

JOHN NEUMANN WAS THE FIRST UNITED STATES BISHOP to be canonized. He immigrated from Bohemia, penniless but with theological studies complete and a knowledge of six languages. Accepted and ordained almost at once by the archbishop of New York, Neumann was sent as pastor to a territory in northern New York more extensive than the whole of his native country. Later he joined the Redemptorists, soon becoming superior of an entire mission band, which allowed him to keep the most difficult work for himself, use a closet under the stairs as his room, and practice poverty of dress. In 1852, John Neumann was consecrated the fourth bishop of Philadelphia. As bishop, he founded fifty churches and more than one hundred schools.

~

On his first visit to take up his post in northern New York, he saw Niagara Falls. Ever after, he referred to this great gush of water as "my baptismal font."

John said: "A man must always be ready, for death comes when and where God wills it."

Charles of Sezze

(d. 1670)

CHARLES WAS RAISED BY HIS GRANDMOTHER who instilled in him a sense of religious fervor. Charles was an unsuccessful student and thus had to abandon his idea of entering the priesthood. Instead, he worked in the fields with his brothers. Then Charles entered the Franciscans and was assigned to a house in Rome where even high-ranking Church officials sought the advice of this simple brother.

~

During the summer months, Friar Diego would call the brother novices into the kitchen after the midnight office and give them lessons in both spirituality and cooking. Whenever Charles made a mistake—and apparently he made quite a few—he was ordered to perform severe penances, such as carrying a heavy stone suspended from his neck throughout the hour or two of work in the kitchen. And if he chanced to say something wrong, he had to lick the kitchen floor from end to end. One afternoon, "the Lord allowed the master to forget" that he had to do this, and Charles licked the kitchen floor for six hours. Charles's only comments was: "It was quite right that that part of my body, which the Lord had given me to honor and bless Him, but with which I had so much offended Him, should receive such a punishment."

Charles was made cook at the San Francesco a Ripa friary; and he felt obliged to give a good lesson to a lay brother who used to come into the kitchen during periods of fasting and consume substantial private snacks. One day Charles said to him firmly, "My friend, don't you think it is more pleasing to the Lord to eat what his charity bestows on us at meal times, rather than to take part in this private satisfaction. The food of the community is made holy by prayer and by the charity of its donors. Can we say as much of what we come and get for ourselves?" These wise words had the desired effect on the snack-addicted friar.

Charles would disregard his own meals—rain, cold, or heat—to try to convert sinners and bring them helpful spiritual advice. For example, a nobleman who had for years lived a life of vice at the court of a certain princess once heard Charles say to him just these words: "Any time, even though late, is pleasing to God."

As a true son of Francis, Charles also extended his compassion to include God's animals. One day when he was lying sick in the infirmary, he noticed a line of ants busily running along a crevice in the window sill. When the brother infirmarian brought his meal, Charles said: "Please give those ants some crumbs, so that these poor creatures may have something to eat."

JANUARY 7
Raymond of Pennafort
(d. 1275)

AFTER AN ILLUSTRIOUS ACADEMIC CAREER, Raymond of Pennafort joined the Dominican Order at the age of forty-seven. Instead of severe penances for which he had asked, his superiors asked him to assemble a collection of cases of conscience to help confessors. Later, the pope asked him to compile all the decrees issued by various popes and Church councils. He was elected master general of the Dominicans, and put through a rule that a superior's voluntary resignation should be accepted. So, after two years in office, he resigned at age sixty-five be-

cause of age. The saint would actually live for thirty-five more years, giving himself to the cause of converting Muslims and Jews.

~

Raymond said this in a letter to a friend: "May the God of love and peace set your hearts at rest and speed you on your journey; may he meanwhile shelter you from disturbance by others in the hidden recesses of his love, until he brings you at last into that place of complete plenitude where you will repose forever in the vision of peace, in the security of trust, and in the restful enjoyment of his riches."

JANUARY 9
Alix le Clercq
(d. 1622)

CO-FOUNDER WITH SAINT PETER FOURIER *of the Augustinian Canonesses Regular of the Congregation of Notre Dame, Alix, as a young woman, indulged in a frivolous lifestyle, but, upon dreaming that Our Lady of Notre Dame, standing beside an altar, beckoned her to come forward, she gave up her fine clothes and began to form plans for an active foundation of women religious. After many difficulties and detours, the pope approved of the young congregation in 1616. Alix died in 1622 at the age of forty-six.*

~

During the founding of this order, Alix was subjected to venomous personal attack and slanderous rumors. She had plenty of opportunity to put into practice her own motto: "I value one act of humility more than a hundred ecstasies."

Marcian of Constantinople

(d. *c*.480)

THOUGH ROMAN, Marcian was a saint of Constantinople. He was ordained a priest and appointed treasurer of Santa Sophia. Many churches were in disrepair in Constantinople but, in his official capacity, Marcian oversaw their restoration, and the building of several new churches. He was also an inspired hymn writer. Marcian gave away much money to the poor—secretly so as not to gain the approval his colleagues.

~

At times he suffered persecution because he was wrongly suspected of being a heretic. One of his persecutors, threatening to kill Marcian, asked him, "Why do you talk of life, if you wish to die?" Marcian replied, "Because it is everlasting life I look for, not the life of this world."

One day when he was hurrying to the consecration of a new church, Marcian passed a miserable, nearly naked beggar. Marcian gave him all his clothing. All he had left was a chasuble. The congregation, however, seemed to see a fine golden robe under Marcian's chasuble. Afterwards Patriarch Gennadius even rebuked the saint for dressing so ostentatiously. Marcian plucked off the chasuble and revealed that he was wearing nothing else.

Vitalis of Gaza
(d. *c*.625)

AT THE AGE OF SIXTY, Vitalis arrived at Alexandria in his monk's habit and assigned himself to work among the prostitutes. To do this, he hired himself out as a laborer and then at night took his wages to one of the woman who worked in that profession. He would give her the money, and say: "I pay you for this that you may spend one night without sin." Then Vitalis would make the woman promise not to reveal the nature of his visit.

∼

One day Vitalis was struck on the head by a man who disapproved of his seemingly sinful behavior. As Vitalis made his way back to his poor hut, the crowd followed. They entered and found Vitalis dead. In his hand was a paper bearing these words: "Judge nothing before the time, until the Lord come, who both will bring to light the hidden things of darkness, and will make manifest the counsels of the heart."

Aelred of Rievaulx
(d. 1167)

AELRED WAS A MEMBER of the household of King David of Scotland. When he was twenty-six, he joined the Cistercian community of Rievaulx in Yorkshire. Gentle with his monks, austere on himself, he reputedly did not dismiss even one of his monks during his seventeen-year tenure as abbot.

∼

Aelred wrote a book entitled *Treatise on Spiritual Friendship*, which begins: "Here we are, you and I, and I hope that Christ makes a third between us."

He defined friendship in this way: "Four things are specially the property of friendship: love and affection, security and joy. And four things must be tried in friendship: faith, intention, discretion, and patience. Indeed, as the sage says, all men would lead a happy life if only two tiny words were taken from them, mine and thine."

JANUARY 13

Hilary of Poitiers
(d. 368)

BORN OF PAGAN PARENTS, Hilary studied rhetoric and philosophy. He married early, had a daughter, and at the age of thirty-five became a Catholic. "I said to myself," he tells us, "that if the present life is not given us to set us on the road to eternal life, then it is not a benefit from God." In 353 he was elected bishop of Poitiers.

～

Hilary wrote a great deal. Here is part of his writer's prayer: "Lord, God Almighty, I owe you, as the chief duty of my life, the devotion of all my words and thoughts. I pray for the gift of your help and compassion, that the breath of your Spirit may fill the sails of my faith, and a favoring wind will be sent to forward me on my voyage of instruction. We shall bring an untiring energy and we shall seek entrance at every gate of hidden knowledge, but it is yours to answer prayer, to grant the thing we seek, to open the door on which we knock. Our minds are born with dull and clouded vision, our feeble intellect is penned within the barriers of an impassible ignorance concerning things divine. We look to you that we may take words in the sense in which they were written and assign the right shade of meaning to every utterance. Grant us therefore precision of language, soundness of argument, grace of style, and loyalty to the truth."

JANUARY 15

Ita of Killeedy

(d. *c.*570)

FOUNDER OF A COMMUNITY *of holy women, Ita is second in popularity to Saint Brigid and is often referred to as the "foster mother of Irish saints" since she taught so many of them in the school she established.*

~

One day a small boy asked Saint Ita to tell him which three things God especially loved. She replied: "True faith in God with a pure heart, a simple life with a religious spirit, openhandedness inspired by charity—these are the three things that God especially loves." "And what," continued the little boy, "are the three things which God most abhors?" "A face," Ita said, "which scowls on all mankind, obstinacy in wrongdoing, and an overweening confidence in the power of money. These are three things hateful to God's sight."

Antony of Egypt

(d. 356)

THE PATRIARCH OF ALL MONKS *and the first of the great desert fathers, Antony, at the age of twenty, gave away his considerable inheritance to the poor and took up the life of a hermit where he was occupied with manual labor, prayer, and religious reading. His only food was bread with a little salt, and he drank nothing but water.*

~

In a search for greater solitude, Antony hid himself in an old tomb in the desert, where a friend brought him a little bread from time to time. Once, he was so severely attacked by devils that when his friend arrived he lay almost dead. As Antony regained consciousness, he called out to the devils, "See, here I am. Do your worst. Nothing shall separate me from Christ my Lord." At this, ghostly beasts in horrible shapes again filled the tomb, until a ray of heavenly light, breaking through, chased them away. "Where were you," Antony cried, "my Lord and my Master? Why were you not here from the beginning of my conflict to give me assistance?" "Antony," replied a voice, "I was here the whole time; I stood by you, and watched your conflict. And because you have manfully withstood your enemies, I will forever protect you and will make your name famous throughout the earth."

During the persecutions under Maximian, Antony went down to Alexandria, openly wearing his white hermit's habit. He went about preaching Christ, and people flocked to hear him. He made many converts and worked several miracles.

The governor of Egypt then invited him to stay, but Antony declined, saying, "Fish die if they are taken from the water; so does a monk wither away if he forsakes his solitude."

JANUARY 18
Deicolus
(d. *c*.625)

BORN IN LEINSTER, IRELAND, Deicolus was one of the twelve disciples of Saint Columbanus who accompanied him to France in 576 and helped to found the great abbey of Luxeuil. Deicolus worked with Columbanus in Austria and Burgundy. When Columbanus was exiled, Deicolus was unable to accompany him and instead set up a forest hermitage where he lived until his death.

~

Though life was not easy, Deicolus was known for the peace and joy that radiated from his soul and could be seen on his face. Columbanus once asked him, "Why are you always smiling?" He simply answered, "Because no one can take God from me."

JANUARY 19
Wulfstan of Worcester
(d. 1095)

WULFSTAN OF WORCESTER was the last of the Anglo-Saxon bishops. He led an austere life of fasting, preaching, and prayer. At first, Wulfstan permitted meat in his diet. But when he was one day distracted from saying Mass by the smell of roasting meat in the kitchen, he forsook eating any flesh in the future.

After the Battle of Hastings, as the Normans spread across the country, appropriating property, despising the Anglo-Saxons as inferior, and taking over bishoprics and abbeys, Wulfstan refused to surrender his cathedral. Among his greatest achievements was his successful crusade against the Irish slave trade. Wulfstan lived to the great age of eighty-seven and died while engaged in his daily practice of washing the feet of twelve poor men.

~

Beloved by all, in the midst of a busy life he cared for all those who sought his help and never turned anyone away from his door. "Troubled by people!" he exclaimed to those who remonstrated with him because he was always so accessible. "Why, that is what I am here for."

Wulfstan was a great church builder, but he had this to say about these efforts: "The men of old, if they had not stately buildings were themselves a sacrifice to God, whereas we pile up stones, and neglect souls."

JANUARY 22

Vincent Pallotti

(d. 1850)

AFTER OVERCOMING LEARNING DISABILITIES, Vincent was ordained and took a doctorate in theology. He was popular as a confessor and, unfortunately, that popularity caused him to be intensely disliked by the other clergy at the Neapolitan church to which he was appointed. Their persecution of him lasted for almost ten years, during which he never complained.

In 1835 Vincent gathered together a group who were committed to evangelization and social justice, in order to organize vocational schools for poor boys. The schools were intended to teach young people marketable skills such as shoemaking, tai-

loring, carpentry, and agriculture. He worked from the premise that holiness is to be found not only in a religious life of prayer and silence but also by filling any need in any part of life wherever one sees it. From this group would evolve the Pallotines, or the Society of Catholic Apostolate.

Father Pallotti died at the age of fifty-five, a death possibly brought on by his habit of giving away of his cloak and his sitting in a cold confessional for many hours.

~

Vincent once wrote to a young professor, "You are not cut out for the silence and austerities of Trappists and hermits. Be holy in the world, in your social relationships, in your work and your leisure, in your teaching duties and your contacts with publicans and sinners. Holiness is simply to do God's will, always and everywhere."

Some of Vincent's sayings are these:

- Since God is perfect in loving man, man must be perfect in loving his neighbor.
- Not the goods of the world, but God. Not riches, but God. Not honors, but God. Not advancement, but God. God always and in everything.
- Remember that the Christian life is one of action; not of speech and daydreams. Let there be few words and many deeds, and let them be done willingly.

John the Almoner
(d. c.619)

PATRIARCH OF ALEXANDRIA IN EGYPT, John entered the religious life after the deaths of his wife and child. The title "almoner" was given to John because he, upon being elected patriarch, distributed the gold found in the church treasury to hospitals, monasteries, and the poor. He died at Carthage.

One day, John observed that several of his parishioners instead of going to Mass on Sundays stood around the churchyard and talked. Instead of going into the church as usual, John hung around outside with the idlers. They looked at one another in surprise since their bishop should have started Mass by that time. After the crowd was reduced to fidgeting in silence, John said, "You are surprised to see me here, but it is nothing unusual. The pastor has to be where the flock is. If you go into the church, I will go into the church."

John forbade all bad-mouthing in his house and avoided all idle conversation. He was aided in this by his appointment of a man to remind him on all occasions: "My lord, your tomb is unfinished; be pleased to give your orders to have it completed, for you know not the hour when death will seize you."

The governor of Alexandria approached John about his desire to charge burdensome new taxes. John opposed this levy and the governor left John in a huff. John sent him a message toward evening saying, "The sun is going to set. Let not the sun set on your anger." This advice influenced the governor and he abandoned the idea of these taxes.

Francis de Sales

(d. 1622)

THOUGH FRANCIS STUDIED LAW, he left these studies to become a priest in 1593. He then became determined to convert the Calvinists of Switzerland back to Catholicism. After three years of futile missionary work, he finally succeeded, using handwritten pamphlets slipped under the doors of homes to get people to listen to him. Francis was made bishop of Geneva, adding greatly to his load of preaching, visiting, and instruction. With Jane Frances de Chantal, he founded the Order of Visitation. His Introduction to the Devout Life *is a spiritual classic.*

~

Francis said: "To be an angel in prayer and a beast in one's relations with people is to go lame in both legs."

As Francis became older, he noted: "I have to drive myself, but the more I try, the slower I go."

Other of Francis's aphorisms include the following:

- Nothing is so strong as gentleness, nothing so gentle as real strength.
- Half an hour's listening is essential except when you are very busy. Then a full hour is needed.
- There was never an angry man who thought his anger unjust.
- He who is fretted by his own failings will not correct them; all profitable correction comes from a calm, peaceful mind.
- The business of finding fault is very easy, and that of doing better very difficult.

When someone praised a certain man as a thinker because he was so quiet, Francis de Sales retorted wisely, "There's nothing more similar to a wise man than a fool who keeps quiet."

Among Francis de Sales's pithy advice: "Do not wish to be anything but what you are, and try to be that perfectly."

Francis was a teacher of good manners. He said: "In my opinion, it is a greater virtue to eat without choice and in the order in which it is set before you, whether it be to your liking or not, than always to choose the worst…since you renounce not only your own taste but your own choice…and this kind of mortification makes no show, inconveniences no one and is singularly suited to life in the world." He also said: "I would have my devout persons, whether men or women, the best dressed of the company but with the least pomp and affectation."

JANUARY 27
Angela Merici
(d. 1540)

AN ORPHAN, *Angela was raised by her wealthy uncle. At thirteen, she became a Franciscan tertiary, sometimes eating only bread, water, and vegetables once a week. From this time onward, she decided to possess nothing—not even a bed—because the Son of Man had nowhere to lay his head.*

On the death of her uncle, Angela returned to her hometown and began giving catechism lessons to the poor children, horrified at the ignorance so many children had of their religion. Angela's success in this enterprise led to an invitation from a wealthy couple to begin a school in Brescia.

During a visit to Rome for the Holy Year 1525, Angela

told Pope Clement VII of a vision she had experienced of the Savior himself calling her by name to create a society of women. The Holy Father gave her permission to form a community.

In Saint Afra's Church at Brescia in 1535, Angela and twenty-eight companions promised before God to devote the rest of their lives to his service. This was the beginning of the Ursuline nuns.

The order had no habit (members usually wore a simple black dress), took no vows, and pursued neither an enclosed nor a communal life; they worked to oversee the religious education of girls, especially among the poorer classes, and to care for the sick. The Ursulines were formally recognized by Pope Paul III four years after Angela's death (1544).

~

Angela's comments on mother love: "Mothers of children, even if they have a thousand, carry each and every one fixed in their hearts, and because of the strength of their love they do not forget any of them. In fact, it seems that the more children they have the more their love and care for each one is increased."

Angela taught kindness to her students: "Be sincerely kind to every one according to the words of our Lord: 'Learn of me, for I am meek and humble of heart.' Thus you are imitating God, of whom it is said: 'He has disposed all things pleasantly.' "

Her management advice includes these words: "If according to times and needs you should be obliged to make fresh rules and change current things, do it with prudence and good advice."

Thomas Aquinas
(d. 1274)

AN ITALIAN DOMINICAN, *Thomas Aquinas taught theology in Paris, producing many theological works, most notably the* Summa Theologica.

~

One day, a colleague asked Thomas, "Hurry, come look out the window, Brother Thomas; over there, it seems as if a cow is flying!"

Thomas, who approached, said, "I see nothing."

Another colleague countered by saying, "You are a simpleton!"

Thomas replied seriously, "That is possible, but I would rather think that a cow could fly than think that a religious could lie."

Despite his early nickname "The Dumb Ox" (because of his girth), Saint Thomas was a man of personal charm. He once wrote that "the special object of temperance is healthy pleasure in the sensation of touch." He also wrote: "No possession is joyous without a companion" and "Notwithstanding the plants and beasts in a garden, a man can be lonely there." Unlike saints who give rise to the impression that anything pleasurable is suspect, Thomas says that "he who abhors pleasures is boorish and ungracious"; and of boorishness itself, he writes that "it is against reason to be burdensome to others, showing no amusement and acting as a wet blanket."

To a friend, Thomas wrote: "Charity is never a waste of time. Tonight I have given up my prayer...to write to you."

He reminds us: "No one can live without delight, and that is why a man deprived of spiritual joy goes over to fleshly pleasures."

JANUARY 29

Sulpicius Severus

(d. *c*.432)

SULPICIUS, WHO WAS A DISCIPLE and biographer of Saint Martin, sent the following letter to his friend, Saint Paulinus:

"I hear that all your cooks have given notice, because, I suspect, they disdained to minister to your unassuming commissariat, so I am sending you a lad from my own kitchen, able to cook the innocuous bean, to serve the modest beetroot dressed with vinegar and sauce, and to make the humble porridge palatable to hungry monks. He is innocent of the use of pepper, and of spices he knows nothing; he is familiar with cumin, and is especially ready with the noisy pestle and mortar, to crush sweet herbs. He has one fault; let him in a garden, and he will cut down everything in reach, and for cutting mallows, he is insatiable. As for keeping himself in firewood, he won't swindle you, but he will burn everything he can get hold of, he will chop it up and will not even hesitate to lay hands on the roof, or the ancient timbers of the house.

With these virtues and foibles, I trust he will be a son to you rather than a servant, since you do not disdain to call the very humblest your children. I would have liked to serve you myself in his stead, but if the wish is on the way to the deed, remember me at your dinners and your cheerful suppers, for it is better to be a servant to you than a master to others."

John (Don) Bosco
(d. 1888)

FOUNDER OF THE SALESIANS, his work after ordination was concentrated solely on the education of boys—to use love as the inducement for study and progress. Later he formed another institute of women to provide for the education of girls.

~

Don Bosco describes his vocation thus: "It's a form of trade, you see. I ask God for souls, and pay him by giving up everything else."

On gentleness, Don Bosco said: "Meekness was the method that Jesus used with the apostles. He put up with their ignorance and roughness and even their infidelity. He treated sinners with a kindness and affection that caused some to be shocked, others to be scandalized, and still others to gain hope in God's mercy. Thus, he bade us to be gentle and humble of heart."

On one occasion, Don Bosco visited a countess who was known to have a big fortune, but a small heart. He knocked on the door of her mansion and said, "Good afternoon, Miss. Is your mother, the countess, at home?"

"But I *am* the countess," the lady answered, perplexed but also pleased.

Don Bosco said, "Now, don't try to fool me. I enjoy speaking with you, Miss, but I really came to see your mother. Is she at home?"

The countess was delighted with the saint's implied compliment and gladly made a larger donation than she had ever been known to make.

February

~

FEBRUARY 1
Brigid of Ireland
(d. c.523)

BRIGID IS VENERATED as a patron saint of Ireland.

~

A story is told that Brigid gave away everything in her own house and her father's house as well. One day, she and her community had spent a long day feeding the poor—when they had given away every loaf of bread, every egg, and every piece of fruit from their fruit trees, announcement was made that a group of bishops would be visiting and would expect their hospitality. The nuns were in despair. What would the bishops think? Brigid, without a blink, told her nuns to "go out and ask the hens kindly to lay more eggs." "Speak to the trees," she said, "see what they have left in the way of fruit." She herself went into the kitchen, and there on the hearth lay loaves of bread, hot and crusty. The chickens gave eggs, the trees dropped fruit into the hands of the sisters, and the bishops declared that they had never sat down to such a fine meal in all their lives.

Francis Mary Paul Libermann
(d. 1852)

FRANCIS LIBERMANN WAS A FRENCH CONVERT from Judaism, missionary, and founder.

~

Francis often gave this advice: "Do things simply, without too much analysis. If you really want to please God and intend to be in full agreement with his will, you can't go wrong."

Ansgar
(d. 865)

KNOWN AS THE APOSTLE OF THE NORTH, Ansgar was born in France and entered a Benedictine monastery after the death of his mother. Ansgar became friends with King Harald of Denmark during that king's exile, returning with him to preach the Gospel in Denmark. He then moved on to Sweden. After an unpromising start, he succeeded in forming the nucleus of a church—the first Christian church in Sweden. His work of fourteen years was destroyed when Vikings overran Scandinavia.

Ansgar was then appointed archbishop of Bremen, but heroically returned to Denmark and Sweden in 854 to start his missionary work all over again. Ansgar often wore a hair shirt, lived on bread and water when his health permitted it, and added short personal prayers to each psalm in his psalter, thus contributing to a form of devotion that soon became widespread.

~

Ansgar once said to a friend: "One miracle I would, if worthy, ask the Lord to grant me; and that is, that by His grace, he would make me a good man."

Gilbert of Sempringham
(d. 1189)

WHILE A PRIEST AT SEMPRINGHAM, Gilbert encouraged seven women to adopt a rule of life based on a Cistercian model. He also founded an order of men whose rule was based on the Augustinian Rule. This is the beginnings of the Gilbertines whose communities in England took the form of double monasteries of both men and women. Gilbert was arrested and charged with sending help to the exiled Thomas à Becket. The charge was false, yet Gilbert chose to suffer imprisonment and risk the suppression of his order, rather than to condemn what was good and just. He died at the age of one hundred six.

～

As master of the Gilbertines, Gilbert always had at his table a dish which he called the Plate of the Lord Jesus, on which he put all the best of what was served up. This plate was given to the poor.

Josepha Rossello
(d. 1880)

FOUNDRESS OF THE DAUGHTERS OF OUR LADY OF MERCY, Josepha spent her ministry teaching the poor, caring for abandoned children, and doing all kinds of charitable works. When she died, there were sixty-eight houses in her order.

Josepha's founding focus is summed up in this statement: "Hands are made for work, and the heart is made for God."

Amandus
(d. *c*.676)

THE APOSTLE OF FLANDERS, Amandus was born in what is now France and spent his early religious life first living at a small monastery and then living in a cell near the cathedral of Bourges. He went on a pilgrimage to Rome and on his return to France he was consecrated bishop with a general instruction to preach the Gospel to the inhabitants of Flanders. Amandus was exiled from France by King Dagobert I for his disapproval of his immoral life. Dagobert, though, begged him to return so that he could baptize his son. Amandus founded numerous monasteries, including the Abbey of Elnon where he spent the last years of his life.

When Amandus first entered a monastery, and had been there for less than a year, his father desperately tried to persuade him to quit that state of life. To his father's threats to disinherit him, Amandus cheerfully replied: "Christ is my only inheritance."

Mary of Providence

(Eugénie Smet) (d. 1871)

FOUNDRESS IN PARIS OF THE HELPERS OF THE HOLY SOULS, Eugénie was born of a relatively prosperous French family. As a student she was inspired to a variety of good works. Encouraged by Saint John Vianney, she organized a congregation dedicated to the poor souls in purgatory and to works of charity here on earth. She died, her cancer an open wound in her side, in 1871 in a cellar in besieged Paris, forced to take refuge there because of the Franco-Prussian War.

~

The story is told of Eugénie that she first discovered human suffering at her family's country house a few miles outside of Lille. There she gained her father's permission to let her take his windfall fruit to the poor. He soon realized that it was not only the wind that was shaking his fruit trees, but his daughter Eugénie as well.

Jacoba of Settesoli

(d. 1239)

A NOBLE ROMAN WOMAN and Third Order Franciscan, Jacoba was the widow of a prominent legislator of that city. She heard Francis of Assisi's message of poverty and penitence when he visited Rome to secure the approval of the pope for his order. Jacoba enthusiastically renounced the world and transferred all her possessions to her two sons. She set up a hospice for sick Franciscans in Rome and provided generously for their needs. After Francis died, Jacoba went to live at Assisi where she spent the remaining days of her life and was laid to rest in the crypt of the lower church of San Francesco near the spot where Francis was buried.

~

As Francis of Assisi lay dying, he sent a notice of the fact to Jacoba as he had promised. But before the letter could be sent, Jacoba arrived in Assisi to sit at his bedside. To Francis she related: "In prayer last evening I heard a voice, which said: 'If you wish to see Brother Francis alive, go at once to St. Mary of the Angels; take with you whatever will be necessary for his burial as well as the refreshments that you used to provide for him when he was ill.' So I came and brought with me ash-gray cloth (to use as a shroud), candles, and honey and almond cakes."

FEBRUARY 9
Teilo
(sixth century)

A WELSH BISHOP, Teilo accompanied Saint David of Wales to Jerusalem and was a friend of Saint Samson during a seven-year stay in France where he planted an orchard of fruit trees that was three miles long. He returned to Wales and founded Llandaff monastery.

~

In reply to a question put to him by Saint Cadoc, Teilo is reputed to have replied: "The greatest wisdom in a man is to refrain from injuring another when it is in his power to do so."

Scholastica

(d. *c.*543)

TWIN SISTER OF BENEDICT OF NURSIA who was founder of the Benedictine Order, Scholastica established a convent for women about five miles south of Monte Cassino, the place where Benedict's monastery was located. Three days after a visit by Benedict, Scholastica died. Benedict sent some monks to fetch her body, which he placed in the tomb he had prepared for himself.

~

Saint Gregory in his *Dialogues* gives an account of the last meeting of Benedict and Scholastica during which they spent the day in talk of God. Benedict prepared to leave. Scholastica, having a premonition that it would be their last opportunity to see each other alive, asked him to spend the evening in conversation. Benedict refused because he did not wish to break his own rule by spending a night away from Monte Cassino. As a result, Scholastica cried openly, laid her head upon the table, and prayed that God would intercede for her. As she did so, a sudden storm arose. The violent rain and hail came in such a downpour that Benedict and his companions were unable to depart.

"May Almighty God forgive you, sister" said Benedict, "for what you have done."

"I asked a favor of you," Scholastica replied simply, "and you refused it. I asked it of God, and he has granted it!"

Humbeline
(d. *c.*1136)

SISTER OF BERNARD OF CLAIRVAUX, Humbeline married a nobleman of the house of Lorraine. With permission from her husband, she entered a convent where she eventually became abbess. Her mortifications there became her way of making up for years of fine living. She died in the presence of three of her brothers.

~

As the wife of a nobleman, Humbeline went to visit Bernard at Clairvaux, dressed in her finest garb and accompanied by a great retinue of servants. Bernard refused to see her until she promised to do as he told her—which was basically to renounce her life of excess. Humbeline burst into tears but had the wit to reply: "I may indeed be a sinful woman, but it was for such as me that Christ died."

Jordon of Saxony
(d. 1237)

A DOMINICAN, considered the second founder of the Order of Preachers, Jordan was in large part responsible for recruiting many young men to join the followers of Saint Dominic.

~

A Saxon, Jordan was a master of that English trait we know as common sense. When asked which is better, studying Scripture or praying, he answered: "You might as well ask which is better—eating or drinking." When asked a question on the best way to pray, he replied: "The best way to pray is the way in which you can pray most fervently."

Jordan was leading a group of young novices in prayer. For some reason, laughter broke out, whereupon an indignant friar became angry with the young men. When it was over, Jordan turned to the aggrieved friar and said, "Who appointed you novice master?" Then he said to the novices: "Laugh on. You have good cause for laughter. For you have escaped from the bondage of the devil. Laugh away, dear sons."

A fellow friar stood opposed to Jordan's plan to readmit a penitent young man who had left the order. Blessed Jordan said to this objector: "If you, my brother, had shed a single drop of your blood for this man for whom Our Lord shed his blood, you would think very differently about this matter." The friar withdrew his objection.

Here is Jordan's recipe for emotional calm: "Sometimes we get unduly elated when things go well, and at other times we are too dejected when they go badly....What we need is to establish our hearts firmly in God's strength, and struggle as best we can to place all our confidence and hope in him; in this way we shall be like him, as far as is possible, even in his unchanging rest and his stability."

Jordan loved poverty. On one occasion he gave his cloak to a beggar who promptly sold it for a drink. "Better," said Blessed Jordan, "a gift wasted than charity refused."

As Jordan walked along on his recruiting trips, he would sing his favorite hymns or would be lost in contemplation. Sometimes he would lose his way. It did not trouble him, for he would always say: "We are on the right road to heaven."

Claude de la Colombière
(d. 1682)

A FRENCH JESUIT, Claude was the spiritual director of Saint Margaret Mary Alacoque whose visions of the Sacred Heart he authenticated. He was sent to England as chaplain to the Duchess of York, bravely enduring anti-Catholic politics. He was caught up in the "Popish Plot" of Titus Oates and was arrested and dragged off to prison. Claude calmly read the breviary as treason charges were read aloud in court. Louis XIV intervened to save him from execution in England and he was banished to France where his health failed. He died peacefully in the south of France.

~

Claude's devotion to the Sacred Heart is expressed in a letter to a dying nun: "Rest assured," he said, "that if I were as near rendering my account to God as you seem to be, it would be precisely the number and gravity of my sins that would serve to quicken my trust. Instead of being cast down by the realization of one's failures, to have a strong and boundless conviction of the Creator's goodness—that is a trust worthy of God. It seems to me that confidence inspired by innocence and purity of life does not give a very great glory to God. Is God's mercy able to do no more than save holy souls who have never offended him? Surely the trust that gives the Lord most honor is that of an errant sinner who is so convinced of God's boundless mercy that all his sins seem like a speck in comparison with that mercy."

Fintan of Clonenagh

(d. 603)

IRISH ABBOT, FINTAN LED THE LIFE OF A HERMIT at Clonenagh, attracting many disciples, including Saint Comgal. He was said to have existed on a diet of barley bread and muddy water. Fintan is a favorite Irish saint and his feast is celebrated throughout Ireland.

∼

The ingenuity of Fintan is expressed in this story: One day some soldiers brought the severed heads of their enemies to the monastery. Fintan had these buried in the monks' cemetery hoping that by Judgment Day they would have benefited from the prayers of generations of monks: "Since the principal part of their bodies rest here, we hope they will find mercy."

Peter Damian

(d. 1072)

BORN AT RAVENNA, THE YOUNGEST CHILD of a poor family, he was orphaned shortly after his birth. He was left in the care of an older brother who gave him the task of herding swine. Another brother took pity on him and paid for his schooling. Afterwards Peter joined the Benedictine community of Fontavellana. He consented to become bishop of Ostia only after being threatened with excommunication for refusing to accept the post. He wrote many theological works, but also Latin verse. Though never formally canonized, Peter Damian was declared a Doctor of the Church in 1828.

∼

Peter gives this advice on obtaining salvation: "The man who is wise and earnestly intent on guarding his salvation watches always with such great solicitude to repress his vices that with the belt of perfect mortification he girds his loins on all sides. This indeed is then done, when the itching palate is repressed, when the bold tongue is restrained in silence, when the ear is closed to evil speaking, when the eye is forbidden to look at illicit things, when the hand is restrained lest it strike cruelly, the foot lest it go off wandering idly; when the heart is resisted lest it envy the good fortune of another's happiness, lest it desire through avarice that which is not its own, lest it cut itself off by wrath from fraternal love, lest it arrogantly praise itself above others, lest it sink immoderately into grief."

Peter advises: "Strengthen your patience with understanding, and look forward serenely to the joy that comes after sadness.

FEBRUARY 22

Margaret of Cortona
(d. 1297)

ABUSED BY A HARSH STEPMOTHER, Margaret sought refuge with a young nobleman. She eloped with him and became his mistress for nine years, always hoping that he would make good on his promise to marry her, especially after she bore him a son. After the murder of her lover, Margaret tried to return to her father's home, but her stepmother refused to admit her because she was such a public sinner. Finally, she went to Cortona, to the Franciscans, who, after she underwent three years of sincere repentance, allowed her to become a member of the Third Order of Saint Francis.

Margaret devoted her energies to prayer and service to the poor, founding a group which staffed a hospital for the poor and gave counsel to prisoners. At the end of her life, Margaret retired to a remote retreat where she lived alone and saw only her priest. She died at age fifty after twenty-nine years of penance.

~

As Margaret grew in holiness, many people came to hear from her a word of comfort. Margaret sent them to the Franciscans, especially to her confessor. He complained that there were too many of these people. Margaret then heard a voice saying: "Your confessor has forbidden you to send him so many men and women who have been converted through your words and tears. He said to you that he could not clean so many stables in one day. Say to him that when he hears confession he does not clean stables; he prepares for me a dwelling in the souls of the penitent."

FEBRUARY 24

Ethelbert of Kent

(d. 616)

KING OF KENT, *Ethelbert's marriage to Bertha, daughter of the Frankish king Charibert, was the occasion of the first introduction of Christianity into Anglo-Saxon England. Probably through Bertha's influence, Ethelbert welcomed Augustine in 597 and he himself was converted the same year, being baptized on Pentecost.*

~

Some days after Augustine's arrival in England, Ethelbert received Augustine at an open-air meeting. When Augustine had preached the Good News to him and his attendants, the king said: "Your words and promises are very fair, but as they are new to us, and of uncertain import, I cannot approve of them so far as to forsake that which I have so long followed with the whole of the English nation. But because you are come from far into my kingdom, and, as I conceive, are desirous to impart to us those things which you believe to be true, and most beneficial, we will not molest you but rather have you as our guest and supply you with the necessary food."

FEBRUARY 26

Porphyry
(d. 420)

TURNING HIS BACK ON FAMILY AND FRIENDS, Porphyry entered a monastery in Egypt but later made his way to Jerusalem because of a series of illnesses. There, leaning on a stick and walking only with grave difficulty, he visited all the places associated with Our Lord's Passion. Porphyry was ordained a priest about the age of forty, and the bishop of Jerusalem committed to his care the relics of the Holy Cross. But, first he divided all his wealth among the poor, and learned to make shoes in order to earn a living. Later he was made bishop of Gaza.

~

While Porphyry was in Jerusalem visiting the holy places, a friend saw him struggling and offered to help him. Porphyry declined the offer, saying: "It is not right that I, who have come here to implore pardon for my sins, should be helped to make my task easier: rather let me undergo some trouble and inconvenience that God, seeing it, may have compassion on me."

Gabriel Possenti of
Our Lady of Sorrows
(d. 1862)

HANDSOME, LIKABLE, AND PLEASURE-LOVING, Gabriel was known as a ladies' man until he fell ill and almost died. Vowing that if he recovered he would enter religious life, Gabriel soon recovered but relapsed and renewed his allegiance to the pleasures of the world. Once again, illness struck and Gabriel renewed his promise, this time fulfilling his vow and astonishing many of his friends. He entered the Passionist Order where he joyously observed all the penances prescribed by its rule. He was ordained but, at the age of twenty-three, he was stricken with tuberculosis and died the next year.

∼

Gabriel wrote this advice to a friend: "If you truly love your soul, shun bad companions; shun the theater. I know by experience how very difficult it is when entering such places in the state of grace to come away with having lost it, or at least exposed it to great danger. Avoid pleasure parties and avoid evil books. I assure you that if I had remained in the world, it seems certain to me that I should not have saved my soul. Tell me, could any one have indulged in more amusements than I? Well, and what is the result? Nothing but bitterness and fear."

Hedwig of Poland
(d. 1399)

DAUGHTER OF LOUIS OF HUNGARY, who claimed both Hungary and Poland, Hedwig was crowned queen of Poland when her father died and when she was only nine years old. She was promised in marriage to the Duke of Austria but chose to marry Jagiello, a non-Christian prince of Lithuania in order to ensure his conversion and secure a measure of peace for Poland. In the years that followed, Hedwig ruled with the king, helping to establish the church in Lithuania and sponsoring the refounding of the university at Krakow, making it a seat of learning in law and theology. Hedwig did not live a long life: her firstborn died at birth and she not long after.

~

When Hedwig was pregnant with her first child, her husband told her of his plan to lavish her with rich jewels and adornments. Hedwig replied: "Seeing that I have so long renounced the pomps of this world, it is not on that treacherous couch—to so many the bed of death—that I would willingly be surrounded by their glitter. It is not by the help of gold or gems that I hope to render myself acceptable to that Almighty Father who has mercifully removed me from the reproach of barrenness, but rather by resignation to his will and a sense of my own nothingness."

$\mathcal{M}$arch

~

MARCH 1
David of Wales
(d. c.560–601)

PATRON SAINT OF WALES, David (or Dewi) became a priest, engaged in missionary activities, and founded twelve monasteries, the last of which, in southwestern Wales, was known for its strict rule. Here David's monks followed a rule of only one daily meal, severe fasts, hours of silence, and hard manual labor. No plow was permitted in the working of the fields, for David said: "Every man is his own ox." David followed the same rigorous discipline: he drank nothing but water and so came to be known as David the Waterman.

~

David was reputed to have a lovable and happy disposition, and a persuasive preaching style. He was, therefore, an obvious choice when the time came for the appointment of a new archbishop of Wales. We are told by his biographer that he opened "many fountains in dry places, and across the centuries his words spoken in the hour of death still reach us: "Brothers and sisters, be joyful.""

Nicholas Owen
(d. 1606)

A CARPENTER, *Nicholas saved the lives of many Jesuit priests in England for two decades by constructing hiding places for them in mansions throughout the country. He became a Jesuit lay brother in 1580, was arrested in 1594 with Father John Gerard, and despite prolonged torture would not give the names of any of his Catholic colleagues; he was released on the payment of a ransom by a wealthy Catholic. Nicholas was arrested again in 1606 with Father Henry Garnet, whom he had served for eighteen years, Father Edward Oldcorne, and Father Oldcorne's servant, Brother Ralph Ashley. Again he refused to give any information concerning priests and lay Catholics. The group was imprisoned in the Tower of London, and Nicholas was subjected to such vicious torture that he died because of it.*

~

Nicholas Owen's hiding places were incredibly sophisticated. At one rural mansion, home to a family of Catholics, he built secret trapdoors in the turrets and stairways, connecting them with the mansion's sewer system. In this way priests could stand up to their waists in water. Owen ran feeding tubes into the hiding places, so that priests secreted within could receive food for the days or weeks that they were sequestered. Sometimes he built an easily discovered outer hiding place which then conceal an inner hiding place. The exact number of hiding places that Owen constructed remains unknown; some still remain hidden.

MARCH 3
Katharine Drexel
(d. 1955)

FOUNDER OF THE SISTERS OF THE BLESSED SACRAMENT whose apostolate is service to Native and African Americans, Katharine was the second daughter of a prominent and wealthy American banking family. By the time of her retirement, she had established over two hundred Catholic missions and schools for Native and African Americans.

~

A newspaper interviewer wrote this about Katharine Drexel: "Her bright blue eyes suddenly twinkled, and she exclaimed with a chuckle: 'Please don't say that I had some great sorrow that drove me into a convent. That's nonsense. I am, and always have been, one of the happiest women in the world. I never had a sorrow in my life except those that must come to men and women who live long enough to outlive many of their loved ones.'"

In a letter to Bishop O'Connor in 1881, Katharine wrote: "I am resolved to eat no cake for 1882, nor preserves until June of this new year, nor grapes nor honey until the first of July, but may I eat chocolates one a year, Reverend Father, for to deny myself such rare treats would surely be the sin of ingratitude."

John of God

(d. 1550)

ORPHANED AS A CHILD, John of God served in the military where he was guilty of many grievous sins. When he was about forty, he became deeply remorseful and decided to dedicate himself to God's service. He initially thought of going to Morocco in Africa to minister to and rescue Christian slaves. That mission was short-lived, and he returned to Granada where he opened a religious goods store.

～

After hearing John of Ávila preach, he was so touched that he ran about the streets behaving like a lunatic. John was taken to an insane asylum, where John of Ávila visited him, telling him that he had practiced his penance long enough and that he should address himself to doing something more useful for himself and his neighbor.

On his release from the hospital, with the help of the archbishop of Granada, John opened a hospital to care for the sickly poor. Those who joined in helping him eventually became the Brothers of Saint John of God. John fell ill after trying to rescue a drowning child from a flooded river. He died on his knees before the altar of his hospital chapel.

John of God knew the value of humor when collecting alms. On his jaunts around town, he shook an old tin can and said happily to passersby: "Do yourselves a good deed, friends, do yourselves a good deed."

The bishop called John of God to him in response to a complaint that he was keeping immoral women in his hospital. In response, John fell on his knees and said: "The Son of Man came for sinners, and we are bound to seek their conversion. I am unfaithful to my vocation because I neglect this, but I confess that I know of no bad person in my hospital except myself alone, who am indeed unworthy to eat the bread of the poor."

MARCH 9
Frances of Rome
(d. 1440)

A BEAUTIFUL CHILD BORN OF WEALTHY PARENTS, Frances begged to be a nun, but her father refused his permission. At the age of twelve, Frances was married in an act of obedience to her father. Almost immediately, however, she became ill and was bedridden for a full year.

~

During her illness, Frances's sister-in-law Vannozza nursed her and they became friends. When Frances learned that Vannozza also had hoped to live as a religious, the two sisters-in-law planned a program of devotions. Duty to family was their first obligation, including running the household with happy hearts and smiling faces.

Frances bore her husband, Lorenzo, a son and two daughters (the daughters died of the plague). Lorenzo, sensing the deep holiness of his wife, promised Frances complete liberty if she would only agree to always inhabit his house. Frances agreed to this. Some years later, Frances told her friends that Christ had commanded her to build a spiritual home. They selected a house and adopted a set of rules. Known as the Oblates of Mary, ten women moved into their house on the feast of the Annunciation; Agnes Selli was chosen as their first superior.

When Lorenzo died peacefully, Frances arranged for Masses to be said for him and settled his estate. She then applied for admission to the community. Agnes wanted to resign as superior, Frances objected but was overruled by the oblates. In March 1440, her son Battista succumbed to a fever, and Frances instantly went to his side. It soon became apparent that she, too, was ill, but, nevertheless she insisted on returning to her community on foot and stopping to ask her spiritual director's blessing. Frances would die in seven days, just as she finished vespers.

Frances of Rome said this about marriage and sanctity: "A married woman, even when praising God at the altar, must when needed by her husband or the smallest member of her family, quit God at the altar and find him again in her household affairs."

MARCH 10
John of Vallumbrosa
(d. c.1380)

JOHN'S ADDICTION TO BOOKS was his undoing. In the course of his studies he was drawn to forbidden books and the secret practice of the Black Arts. When discovered by his abbot-general, at first he denied his sin, but finally he confessed, was found guilty, and imprisoned. During his internment, he truly repented and voluntarily undertook vigorous fasting almost to the point of starvation. Eventually, he was asked to return to his community; he, however, chose to remain in prison until his death at a very old age.

～

In his solitude, John attained great sanctity, saying: "I have learned in this long imprisonment, that there is nothing better, nothing more holy than solitude: In solitude I intend to go on learning divine things and to try to rise higher. Now that I am free from temporal fetters I am resolved, with the help of Christ, to waste no more time."

MARCH 11 heading

MARCH 11

Eulogius of Cordova
(d. 859)

IN 850, the Moors of Spain began a systematic persecution of the Christians, probably because of attempted evangelization of Muslims by Christians. Ordained a priest, Eulogius was one of those arrested. A few days later, however, he was released. During the next seven years of this persecution, Eulogius worked tirelessly to bolster the spirits of his fellow Christians. Eulogius was elected archbishop of Toledo, but never set foot in his diocese. In 859, he was again arrested and was martyred for protecting Lucretia, a convert from Islam, who was condemned to death for becoming a Christian.

~

In Eulogius's *Exhortation to Martyrdom* he addressed two young ladies imprisoned with him: "They threaten to sell you as slaves and dishonor you, but be assured that they cannot injure the purity of your souls, whatever infamy they may inflict upon you. Cowardly Christians will tell you in order to shake your constancy that the churches are silent, deserted, and deprived of the sacrifice on account of your obstinacy. But be persuaded that for you the sacrifice most pleasing to God is contrition of heart, and that you can no longer draw back or renounce the truth you have confessed."

Louis Orione

(d. 1940)

As a young boy, Louis went to the Salesian Oratory at Turin where he was accepted by Don Bosco as one of the group whose confessions he heard regularly. This experience led to his decision to enter the diocesan seminary of Tortona where he was ordained at the age of twenty-three. Louis's youthful energy and intelligence was directed toward the underprivileged, the sick, and the suffering. He serenaded prisoners with his mandolin, visited the hospitals, organized catechism classes and sports for the young boys of the neighborhood. These works of charity were the beginning of his blueprint for the Congregation of the Little Work of Divine Providence. His "work" was to hold out a helping hand to all who needed food, a bed, or words of comfort. Louis died in 1940 and a prayer set down in his notebook echoes the spirit of his apostolate: "Lord, set me down at the gates of hell so that by your mercy I may keep them shut against all comers."

~

When the honor of having Don Bosco hear his confession was given to Louis, he prepared for it by filling three exercise books with his sins. "What will Don Bosco have to say when he reads all this," Louis thought. When his turn arrived, he knelt at Don Bosco's feet. Don Bosco looked at him and smiled. "Give me your sins."

Out came the first exercise book. Don Bosco took it, felt it for a moment as if to test its weight, and then tore it into pieces. "Now give me the others," Don Bosco said. These too were torn to shreds.

Louis was stunned. Then he remembered: Of course, Don Bosco reads consciences. He has no need of written words.

"That's the end of this confession," said the priest. "Never give another thought to anything that you have written down here."

Clement Mary Hofbauer
(d. 1830)

BAKER, HERMIT, PREACHER, REFORMER, Clement joined the Redemptorist Order and was sent to establish its presence in Poland. There he built orphanages and schools, but after two decades of missionary labor, Clement was exiled to Vienna, where he became chaplain to the Ursulines and pastor of the adjoining church. Here he helped to revitalize the Catholic faith in Austria and Germany.

~

One day, Clement was collecting money for his orphanage. He wandered into a tavern and asked if anyone would care to make a donation. One man took a big mouthful of beer and spat it right into the saint's face. Clement calmly wiped his face, saying, "That was for me. Now are you going to give something for my orphans?" His quiet humor worked and all the people in the tavern gave Clement generous donations.

Clement was kneeling in the sanctuary, praying for a special favor. Remembering Our Lord's words about perseverance in prayer, he suddenly climbed the steps to the altar, rapped on the tabernacle, and said, "Lord, we'll see who gives up first."

Finnian Lobhar

(d. *c.*560)

AN IRISH ABBOT, Finnian is believed to have built a church at Innisfallen in County Kerry. Later he lived at Clonmore Abbey in Leinster and then went to Swords near Dublin, where he was made abbot by Columba. People flocked to Finnian to be cured of their diseases.

~

Lobhar means "the Leper," a name he acquired when a woman brought her small boy, who was blind, mute, and a leper, and prayed that Finnian might effect a cure. In a revelation Finnian was told that if he wished his prayer answered then he must take on the leprosy himself. He cheerfully agreed, and was covered with ulcerated sores from the top of his head to the bottoms of his feet.

Gertrude of Nivelles

(d. 659)

BENEDICTINE ABBESS, GERTRUDE IS REMEMBERED for her hospitality, especially to pilgrims and missionaries. She resigned her post as abbess when she was thirty years old and spent the rest of her days studying Scripture and doing penances. She died at the age of thirty-three, the same age at which Our Lord was crucified.

~

Gertrude is associated with many customs. She is sometimes shown with mice which represent the souls in purgatory to whom she had a great devotion. She is the patron saint of gardeners because fine weather on her feast day was interpreted to mean it was time to begin spring planting. Her patronage of travelers comes from her reputation for hospitality; pilgrims used to drink a toast in her honor before setting out on their journey. Because it was supposed that those who had just died were on a three-day journey to the next world, Gertrude was invoked as a patroness of the recently deceased. It was thought that they spent the first night under the care of Gertrude, and the second under Michael the Archangel.

MARCH 18

Cyril of Jerusalem

(d. 386)

PRIEST, TEACHER, AND GREAT INSTRUCTOR *of catechumens, Cyril became bishop of Jerusalem and was exiled three times by the Arians. He is a Doctor of the Western Church.*

～

Cyril is the author of twenty-four lectures on the Creed, the Our Father, and the Easter sacraments. Here are some excerpts:

It is not only among us, who are marked with the name of Christ, that the dignity of faith is great; all the business of the world, even of those outside the Church, is accomplished by faith. By faith, marriage laws join in union persons who were strangers to each other. By faith, agriculture is sustained; for a man does not endure the toil involved unless he believes he will reap a harvest. By faith, seafaring men, entrusting themselves to a tiny wooden craft, exchange the solid element of the land for the unstable motion of the waves. Not only among us does this hold true but also, as I have said, among those outside the fold. For though they do not accept the Scriptures but advance certain doctrines of their own, yet even these they receive on faith.

Our actions have a tongue of their own; they have an eloquence of their own, even when the tongue is silent. For deeds prove the lover more than words.

MARCH 19

Marcel Callo
(d. 1945)

MARCEL WAS BORN ON DECEMBER 6, 1921, *in Rennes, France, one of nine children. When he was thirteen, Marcel was apprenticed to a printer. He also joined the Christian Worker's Youth organization. After the Nazi invasion of France, Marcel and some friends would go to the railway station and help refugees who were hungry or confused. They were also able to help many people escape arrest by the Nazis by giving the refugees their Red Cross armbands. In March 1943, he was sentenced to slave labor in Nazi Germany where Marcel, although ill himself due to hard work and poor diet, organized the Christian workers and encouraged his fellow prisoners. He was even able to arrange to have a Mass said. The Gestapo viewed this as being "too Catholic." Marcel was arrested and in October 1944 was sent to prison where inmates worked at an underground aircraft factory with inadequate food, clothing, and shelter. He continued to pray and encourage his fellow prisoners. On March 19, 1945, Marcel died from malnutrition.*

∼

Marcel's deportation to Germany was accompanied by toothaches, food poisoning, colic, and fingers that had been damaged in an accident. He was physically and morally depressed. He referred to this time of trial in the following words: "The two months after my arrival were extremely hard. I had no taste for anything. I was without feeling. I was conscious of opting out little by little. Suddenly Christ made me snap out of it. He made me understand that what I was doing was not good. He told me to get on and see to my comrades. Then my cheerfulness returned."

MARCH 21
Nicholas of Flue
(d. 1487)

SOLDIER, FARMER, AND MEMBER OF THE LOCAL PARLIAMENT, Nicholas von Flue condemned wars of aggression and the slaughter of non-combatants as immoral. Somewhere around thirty he married a farmer's daughter, Dorothy Wiss. The couple had ten children. Held in high esteem by his neighbors, he was asked to become mayor of his canton. This he steadfastly refused, saying, "One is safer below than on the heights."

~

Nicolas's active life belied a more contemplative existence of prayer and fasting. His eldest son said this about his father: "My father always retired at the same time as his children and servants, but every night I saw him get up again and heard him praying in his room until morning."

After twenty years of married life, Nicholas, with the consent of his wife decided to become a hermit at Ranft within a few miles of his home. After a month, his countrymen realized the genuineness of his vocation, and he became a spiritual guide whose advice was widely sought and followed. Nicolas died on his seventieth birthday.

Nicolas is seen as the patron saint of Switzerland by both Protestants and Catholics alike. This honor arose because of his peace-making abilities. The cantons of Switzerland were at loggerheads, and a conference held at Stans in December 1481 failed to reach a resolution. On the next day, the delegates would disperse and a civil war would most probably ensue, destroying the Swiss confederacy. A parish priest hurried to Nicolas and entreated his help. During the night Nicholas dictated suggested terms of agreement. The priest returned in time to persuade the delegates to give a hearing to the proposals of this widely respected man. The terms were accepted and war was averted.

MARCH 24
Catherine of Vadstena
(d. 1381)

FOURTH OF THE EIGHT CHILDREN of Saint Bridget and her husband, Ulf Gudmarsson, Catherine was sent to a convent to be educated at a very young age. She was married at age thirteen or fourteen to Eggard Lydersson von Kürnen, a lifelong invalid. She and Eggard took a vow to remain celibate and she tended to him with great devotion.

~

When Catherine's mother, Saint Bridget, went to live in Rome, Catherine traveled there to visit her. While in Rome Bridget learned of her husband's death.

Soon Catherine was her mother's devoted assistant, and served her for the next twenty-five years. In 1373, Saint Bridget died, and Catherine returned with her mother's body to Sweden. There she became abbess of the convent of Vadstena, the motherhouse of the Bridgettine Order founded by her mother. She devoted her life to the promotion of the Bridgettine Order and died soon after she gained its papal approval.

Catherine and her mother, Bridget, had a period of disagreement where Bridget refused to let Catherine leave their Roman quarters for fear of her safety. Catherine was drawn by deep affection for her mother, who wanted her to stay in Rome and assist her, and her desire for the cooling summers of Sweden as a relief from the stifling heat of Rome. She said: "I live a wretched life here, caged like an animal, while the others go and nourish their souls in church. In Sweden my brothers and sisters are allowed to serve God in peace."

MARCH 26
Ludger of Utrecht
(d. 809)

MONK, PRIEST, AND PUPIL of Saint Gregory and Alcuin of York, Ludger took the Gospel to the Netherlands, building churches and converting many. His efforts, however, were undone by the Saxon leader, Widekund, who invaded, destroying Christian foundations and driving out all the missionaries.

∼

Ludger took the opportunity to make a pilgrimage to Rome and also spent two years at the great Benedictine foundation at Monte Cassino. Returning to Westphalia in 786, Emperor Charlemagne charged him with the spiritual care of five provinces. Ludger based himself in a place which was later known as Münster because of the abbey founded there, which followed the Rule of Saint Chrodegang of Metz. His gentleness did more to attract the Saxons to Christ than did all the armies of Charlemagne. After turning down offers of bishoprics, Ludgar finally became the first bishop of Münster. Although suffering from a painful final illness, Ludger continued to preach until the very end of his life.

Accused of excessive almsgiving, Ludger was summoned to appear before Charlemagne. A servant came to summon him into the presence of the emperor, but found Ludger at prayer. Ludger sent back word that he would appear when he had finished his devotions. A second and a third message was sent before Ludger was ready to attend to Charlemagne. When he appeared, Charlemagne asked him why he had not immediately obeyed his summons. Ludger replied: "Because I believed that the service of God was to be preferred to yours or to that of any man. Such indeed was your will when you invested me with the office of bishop and therefore I deemed it unseemly to interrupt the service of God, even at the command of your majesty."

MARCH 27
John of Egypt
(d. c.395)

JOHN WAS A SHOEMAKER-TURNED-HERMIT. When he was about forty, John walled himself into a cell on the top of a rock near Asyut, where he never ate until after sunset. Weekdays he spent his time in prayer. On Saturdays and Sundays, he spoke through the little window in his cell to the many people who came to him for instruction and spiritual advice.

～

John's gift for foretelling the future was held in such high regard that he was given the name "Prophet of the

Thebaid." For example, John foretold the victory of Theodosius over Maximus, as well as the events of other wars, and the incursions of barbarians.

Toward the end of his life, John was visited by Petronius along with six other monks. John asked if any of the visitors were in holy orders and they answered, "no." In fact, Petronius was a deacon but had not disclosed this to his fellow travelers out of a false sense of humility because he was the youngest in the company. When John pointed to Petronius and said, "This man is a deacon," Petronius denied it. John took the younger man's hand and kissed it, while saying: "My son, take care never to deny the grace you have received from God, lest humility betray you into a lie. We must never lie, under any presence of good whatever, because no untruth can be from God."

MARCH 27
Rupert of Salzburg
(d. 720)

AN INTELLIGENT AND VIRTUOUS MAN with a gift to heal bodies and soothe souls, Rupert eventually became the Bishop of Worms (Germany) from which he began his missionary work that stretched across both Germany and Austria. Finally deciding to make his headquarters at Salzburg, he died on Easter Sunday, just after Mass. Until today, September 24, Saint Rupert's Day, has remained the main public holiday in Salzburg. As in centuries before, a fair called the "Ruperti Kirtag" is held which, in former times, attracted buyers and sellers from as far away as London and Constantinople.

~

Unlike many of his contemporaries, he did not destroy pagan temples, but consecrated them as Christian churches. His comments: "Why waste the buildings? If we are to have converts, we must quickly have a place for them to gather and worship. What is quicker than this?" It is said that God affirmed his actions through the granting of numerous miracles.

MARCH 30

John Climacus
(d. *c.*650)

A SYRIAN ABBOT AND WRITER, John authored The Ladder to Paradise. *He joined the monastery of Mount Sinai, spending his novitiate under the supervision of Martyrius. There he learned to forego the need to discuss everything, usually a mark of pride. Instead he adopted humility and obedience, never disputing with anyone. After four years of training, he was professed.*

~

From the age of thirty-five, John spent many years as a hermit at the foot of Mount Sinai, where he studied the Scriptures and the lives of the Fathers of the Church. He practiced fasting, nights of prayer, and abstinence from meat and fish. He became known especially for his ability to comfort the distressed and distracted. When some accused him of spending too much time talking, he kept complete silence for a year until the accusers begged him to resume giving counsel. He died in his hermitage on Mount Sinai.

Here are some of the spiritual maxims from Saint John's book:

- Rule your own heart as a king rules over his kingdom, but be subject above all to the supreme ruler, God himself.
- A person is at the beginning of a prayer when he succeeds in removing distractions which at the beginning beset him. He is at the middle of the prayer when the mind concentrates only on what he is meditating and contemplating. He reaches the end when, with the Lord, the prayer enraptures him.
- Without weapons there is no way of killing wild animals. Without humility there is no way of conquering anger.
- It is not without risk that one climbs up a defective ladder. And so with honor, praise, and precedence which are all dangerous for humility.
- In an instant many are pardoned for their mistakes, but no one, in a moment's time, acquires calmness of the soul which requires much time, much trouble and a great deal of help from God.
- The one who is dead can no longer walk. The one who despairs can no longer be saved.
- A small fire is enough to burn down an entire forest; a little hole may destroy an entire building.
- Just as clouds hide the sun so bad thoughts cast shadows over the soul.
- Birds which are too heavy cannot fly very high. The same is true of those who mistreat their bodies.
- A dried-up puddle is of no use for the pigs and a dried up body is of no use to the devils.

Acacius

(d. *c.*251)

ACACIUS, MUCH-ADMIRED BISHOP OF ANTIOCH, *was sum-moned for investigation during the persecution of Christians under the Emperor Decius. Acacius appeared and began by insisting that his flock was entirely faithful to the emperor. The investigator responded that the saint should prove this by making sacrifice to the emperor as a god. This the bishop resolutely refused to do. Finally Acacius was required to give the names of other Christians. He said: "I am on trial and you ask for names. If you cannot overcome me alone, do you suppose you would be successful with the others? You want names—all right: I am called Acacius, and I have been surnamed Agathangelus. Do what you like." Acacius was then returned to prison and a copy of the proceedings forwarded to the emperor Decius, who, we are told, could not keep from smiling when he read them. There is no evidence that Acacius was actually martyred.*

~

Elsewhere in the interrogation Acacius said: "You make your own gods and are afraid of them. When there are no masons or when the masons have no stone, then you have no gods. We stand in awe of our God but we did not make Him; He made us. For He is our Master, and he loves us, for He is also our Father. In His goodness, He has rescued us from everlasting death."

April

APRIL 2
Francis of Paola
(d. 1507)

KNOWN AS A MIRACLE WORKER, Francis founded an order whose rule is based on penance, charity, and humility and whose goal is to convert people to Christianity particularly through example. Known as the Minims, members of this order were required to abstain from meat, eggs, and anything made from milk. In 1481, Francis was ordered by the pope to travel to the court of King Louis XI of France to comfort the monarch who was dying of the consequences of a stroke. He traveled barefoot to the court and there continued to live a life of simplicity and solitude.

Francis wrote a letter to his followers when he departed for France: Among his advice was these words: "Obey with humility your superiors, for obedience is the backbone of faith. Be sympathetic to the weakness and failings of others. It is vain to begin a good action until you bring it to completion."

Isidore of Seville

(d. 636)

BROTHER OF THREE SAINTS, *Isidore was made bishop of Seville in the year 600. He is sometimes called the "schoolmaster of the Middle Ages," because his writings (especially his* Etymologies—*an encyclopedia of the knowledge of his time) served as textbooks until the sixteenth century.*

Isidore celebrated his death by giving away all his possessions and publicly asking for forgiveness after he had been dressed in sackcloth and anointed with ashes by two of his friends.

~

Isidore encouraged the study of theology and the Scriptures, writing in *The Book of Sentences:* "If anyone wants to be always with God, he ought to pray often and to read often as well. For when we pray, it is we who talk to God, whereas when we read, it is God who speaks to us....The more conscientious one is in becoming familiar with the sacred writings, the richer an understanding one will draw from them, as with the earth—the more it is cultivated, the more abundant is its harvest."

Isidore explains the seeming success of evil persons: "We ought to sorrow for people who do evil rather than for people who suffer it. The wrongdoing of the first leads them further into evil. The others' suffering corrects them from evil. Through the evil wills of some, God works much good in others."

Vincent Ferrer
(d. 1419)

A SPANISH DOMINICAN, Vincent Ferrer was a roving mission-
ary who evangelized in Spain, France, Italy, Germany, England,
Scotland, and Ireland. He turned from supporting the schis-
matic pope at Avignon to actively working toward restoring
the papacy to Rome.

~

Vincent condemns pointless pride, saying: "Whoever proudly disputes and contradicts will always stand outside the door. Christ, the master of humility, reveals his truth only to the humble, and hides himself from the proud."

Vincent's book on the spiritual life gives this advice: "Do you desire to study to your advantage? Let devotion accompany all your studies, and study less to make yourself learned than to become a saint. Consult God more than your books, and ask him with humility to make you understand what you read. Study fatigues and drains the mind and heart. Go from time to time to refresh them at the feet of Jesus under his cross."

John-Baptist de la Salle
(d. 1719)

JOHN-BAPTIST DE LA SALLE USED HIS FORTUNE to set up free
schools for the poor and to found the Brothers of the Christian
Schools who would dedicate themselves to teaching. Among
other works directed to his brothers, John-Baptist wrote The

Rules of Christian Politeness, A Manual of Piety for Schools, The Conduct of Schools, *and* The Duties of A Christian. *John-Baptist was an innovator insofar as he encouraged the training of students in their native language instead of Latin, adjusted for individual differences in learning, proposed whole-class teaching instead of the one-on-one instruction popular at that time, argued for a sequence of curriculum skills, and gave rules for the teaching of reading. In the later part of his life, he was a model of perfect obedience to his successor, so much so that Brother Barthélemy joked that John would not even die without his permission.*

~

Here is an example of de la Salle's expectations for his colleagues and his students: "Adapt yourself with gracious and charitable compliance to all your neighbor's weaknesses. In particular, make it a rule to hide your feelings in many inconsequential matters. Give up all bitterness toward your neighbor, no matter what. And be convinced that your neighbor is in everything better than you....Each day look for every possible opportunity to do a kindness for those you do not like. After examining yourself on this matter every morning, decide what you are going to do, and do it faithfully with kindness and humility."

APRIL 8
Julia Billiart
(d. 1816)

FOUNDER, AFTER THE FRENCH REVOLUTION, of the Sisters of Notre Dame of Namur, Julie was an invalid for almost twenty-two years as a result of the shock of seeing her father shot as she was sitting next to him. Julia was miraculously able to walk on the feast day of the Sacred Heart. Despite her paralysis and

*the disorder of the French Revolution, Julie was seen as a kind
and loving person: One of the early Sisters said of her: "She
was happy and liked to see us happy too, so she made us laugh."*

~

Julie was known for her intelligence which could grasp
the implications of a situation and give an opinion that was
sound and sane. She laid down general principles but did
not dictate the details: She wrote to one superior: "I simply
will not lay down the law about such things. No, no, no, no.
I will go on saying 'no' until tomorrow if you like!" At another time she said, "Go, go, go on, make up your own mind.
Better mistakes than paralysis." And she also wrote, "There
must be no looking back on the past, no anxieties about the
future."

APRIL 8
Maria Magdalen of Canossa
(d. 1835)

*BORN INTO A WEALTHY VERONESE FAMILY, Magdalen was left
fatherless when she was five years old. Her mother abandoned
her upon her remarriage and she was raised by governesses.
When the two elderly uncles for whom she was caring died, she
finally felt free to undertake a "really big project"—to institute
a school that would provide practical education for a large number of girls, especially those who were poor. This was the start
of the Congregation of the Daughters of Charity or the
Canossian Sisters of Charity. As death neared, Magdalen received the last rites, joined in the prayers, and died with an
exclamation of joy. At the last, she was leaning on the arm of
Mother Annetta, to whom, years before, when Annetta was
just a girl, Magdalen had said: "One day you will be one of us
and you will be there to help me when I die."*

~

Maria Magdelen often advised her Sisters: "Be happy… after having experienced Mary's help on so many occasions, how can you be worried or afraid?"

APRIL 11
Guthlac
(d. 714)

A SOLDIER FOR NINE YEARS in the army of King Ethelred, Guthlac gave up his violent life and became a monk in a Benedictine abbey at Repton. He was known for his extraordinary discipline, and many of the monks disliked him because he refused all alcohol. Finally he left the abbey for a more remote spot on the river Wellend, and he lived there for the rest of his life. Despite his isolation and austerities, his biographer said that no one had ever seen him angry or sad.

~

Guthlac was patient even with the birds who stole his few possessions. A holy man once visited Guthlac and was astonished when two birds landed on his shoulders and then hopped all over him. Guthlac told him: "Those who choose to live apart from other humans become the friends of wild animals; and the angels visit them, too—for those who are often visited by men and women are rarely visited by angels."

Peter Gonzalez

(d. 1246)

A CASTILIAN OF NOBLE BIRTH, Peter indulged in a worldly youth, even while he was being educated to take over as the religious role of canon of Palencia. After his under-age appointment, he paraded through town on horseback to impress his new flock. In the noise and excitement, the horse reared and threw Peter into the mud.

~

When his wounded feelings had been healed, Peter reformed his life and entered a Dominican monastery. He did his best to convince his friends to follow him in the religious life. He said: "If you love me, follow me. If you cannot follow me, forget me!" He devoted much of the rest of his life to preaching in the rural areas of Spain.

Peter Gonzalez's favorite saying was this: "Better to live one day in the house of the Lord than to live a thousand in the pavilions of sinners."

Bernadette Soubirous

(d. 1879)

THE OLDEST CHILD of an impoverished miller, Bernadette was fourteen years old when the Immaculate Virgin appeared to her at Lourdes. In 1866, Bernadette was sent to the Sisters of Notre Dame in Nevers. There she became a member of the community and endured some harsh treatment by the novice mistress until it was discovered that she had an incurable dis-

ease. Bernadette desired to remain hidden and forgotten, comparing herself to a broom: "Our Lady used me. They have put me back in my corner. I am happy there and remain there." Bernadette died at the age of thirty-five.

~

Bernadette disliked publicity, but she did not want to remain aloof if a glimpse of her would help another human soul—but sometimes she discharged this self-imposed requirement in a clever way. Once a visitor stopped her as she was passing down a corridor and asked where she could get a glimpse of Sister Bernadette. The little nun said, "Just watch that doorway and presently you will see her go through." And then she slipped away through the door.

Bernadette also managed to find kind and witty answers to the most banal of questions. For example, to questioners who wanted to know how many folds were in the veil of the Madonna, she replied: "How can I remember all the details? If you really want the answers call the Madonna back."

Bernadette tried her best to avoid ecclesiastical visitors. She was once chastised for being reluctant to see a local bishop. Reminded that there was a forty-day indulgence for kissing his ring, she replied: "Jesus, Mary, Joseph, I give you my heart and my soul. There, that gives me one hundred days." And she scampered off.

APRIL 18

Mary of the Incarnation

(Barbara Acarie) (d. 1618)

THOUGH CLEARLY A YOUNG WOMAN OF PIETY, Barbara agreed to marry, saying: "If I am unworthy through my sins to be the bride of Christ, I can at least be his servant." She and her husband had six children; three of her daughters became Carmelite nuns and one of her sons became a priest.

～

Barbara was known throughout Paris for her good works, her visitation of the sick, her ministrations to the poor and the dying. When her husband died, she entered the convent, taking the name Mary of the Incarnation.

As she lay dying, her fellow nuns gathered at her bedside. She prayed: "Lord, forgive me for the bad example that I have set."

APRIL 19

Alphege of Canterbury

(d. 1012)

ALPHEGE WAS TAKEN PRISONER by invading Danes who demanded a huge ransom for the bishop of Canterbury. Alphege refused to burden his people with this request for money and so was murdered by a drunken mob while he was being held captive.

～

Alphege wrote these words while being held in captivity: "I am ready at once for anything you now dare to do to me, but, by the love of Christ, that I may become an example to his servants, I am untroubled today....This my body, which in this exile I have loved immoderately, I offer to you, guilty as it is...but as a suppliant I commit my soul to the creator of all, for it does not concern you."

APRIL 20

Agnes of Montepulciano
(d. 1317)

AT AGE OF NINE, Agnes was allowed by her well-to-do parents to enter a convent popularly called the Order of the Sack for their austere habits. At the age of fifteen, she became prioress of their monastery at Proceno. For years Agnes lived on bread and water and slept on the ground, using a stone as a pillow. At the request of the citizens of Montepulciano, her native town, she established a convent of Dominican nuns at her birthplace and governed it until her death at the age of forty-nine. Saint Catherine of Siena was thought to have been a pilgrim to the shrine of Saint Agnes, and a story is told that when Catherine stooped to kiss the foot of Agnes's incorrupt body, the foot rose up to meet her lips so she would not have to stoop so far.

~

On her deathbed, Agnes, with her usual sweet smile, said this to her grieving nuns: "Do not grieve over much at my departure: I shall not lose sight of you. You will find that I have not abandoned you and you will possess me forever."

Anselm of Canterbury
(d. 1109)

MONK, ARCHBISHOP, AND DOCTOR OF THE CHURCH, *Anselm entered the monastery at Bec in Normandy after a dissolute young adulthood. While there, he wrote a major work on the proofs of the existence of God, as well as treatises on free will, truth, and the origin of evil. He was forcibly made Archbishop of Canterbury and because of political pressure was exiled abroad several times. He finally reached an agreement with the English king whereby the crown would renounce its right of investiture to bishoprics or abbeys, while the bishops would pay homage to the king for their temporal possessions. He died in 1109.*

~

While at Bec, Anselm wrote this to a neighboring abbot, who was concerned about his poor record in training the young: "If you planted a tree in your garden, and bound it on all sides, so that it could not spread out its branches, what kind of a tree would it prove when in after years you gave it room to spread? Would it not be useless, with its boughs all twisted and tangled?…But that is how you treat your boys…cramping them with fears and blows, debarring them from the enjoyment of any freedom."

Anselm also observed: "God often works more by the illiterate seeking of the things that are God's than by the learned seeking the things of their own."

Theodore of Sykeon

(d. 613)

THEODORE'S INFANCY WAS INAUSPICIOUS: he was the son of a circus performer and a prostitute. However, his mother had him baptized. Later, the family's fortunes changed with the arrival of a man whose cooking abilities transformed their inn from a pleasure house into a place renowned for its cuisine. In addition, he encouraged Theodore's tendency to holiness. Theodore became a monk and led a penitential life: he lived on uncooked vegetables seasoned with salt and vinegar, fasted frequently, wore an iron girdle, and lived in an iron cage suspended above the entrance to his hermitage. Theodore was also instrumental in promoting devotion to Saint George.

～

A biography of Theodore written in the seventh century tells this story: Theodore gave orders to some carpenters to make a wooden chest for storing corn. He also commanded them not to touch any meat until the work was finished. (Meat was never eaten in the monastery all the year through.) A few days later when Theodore left to visit a neighboring town, the foreman of the carpenters brought in some meat and secretly ate it, whereupon he was immediately stricken with fever and lay half-dead. When Theodore heard this news he said: "Obedience is life. Disobedience is death. The man has disobeyed my injunction and eaten meat in the monastery and that is the reason why he is ill!" Theodore returned to his monastery and said to the sick man: "Do not conceal from me what you really did, brother; for you ate meat, did you not?" and the foreman answered that that was so. Theodore replied: "Now see and recognize that it is not God who sends wrath upon us, but we who bring it upon ourselves. Rise now in the name of Jesus Christ." Then he blessed him and the man was at once relieved of the fever.

APRIL 23
Giles of Assisi
(d. 1262)

AN EARLY COMPANION OF FRANCIS OF ASSISI, who called this simple brother "our Knight of the Round Table," he went with Francis on his preaching ventures, including trips to Compostela in Spain, the Holy Land, and Tunis to evangelize the Saracens. Though he lacked formal learning, he was often approached for advice by people, and the short sayings attributed to him were collected into a small book.

～

Here is a sampler of Blessed Giles's sayings: On spirituality, "He who does not know how to pray does not know God"; on getting along with others: "If you love, you will be loved. If you fear, you will be feared. If you serve, you will be served"; on human nature: "Blessed is he who does good to others and desires not that others should do good to him."

APRIL 24
Fidelis of Sigmaringen
(d. 1622)

TRAINED IN PHILOSOPHY AND LAW, Fidelis became known as the "Poor Man's Lawyer" because of his work on behalf of the oppressed. Disgusted by the fraud involved in the legal system, Fidelis entered the Capuchins and became a missionary to the

Protestants. He was so successful at this endeavor that he aroused the antagonism of the peasants who thought he was opposing their quest for independence. While he was preaching a sermon on "One Lord, One Faith, One Baptism," he was shot at by a Protestant whose bullet missed. On he way home, he was set upon by twenty soldiers who killed him with their swords, after first trying vainly to make him renounce his faith.

~

When Fidelis was placed as head of the missionaries to the Protestants in Switzerland, he wryly started signing his letters: "Fidelis, who will soon be food for the worms." Fidelis was also an opponent of lukewarmness, saying "Woe is me if I should prove myself but a half-hearted soldier in the service of my thorn-crowned Captain!"

APRIL 26
Richarius
(d. c.645)

WHILE STILL A PAGAN, Richarius protected two Irish missionaries who were in danger of being killed by the people to whom they were preaching. While in hiding with them, they converted him. Richarius became a priest, studying in England. When he returned to France he traveled about the country, preaching the Gospel and healing the sick. He gave up riding on horseback on his journey; instead he rode on a donkey whose slow pace allowed him to say his psalter. Richarius became so well known that King Dagobert I visited him at the monastery which he had founded. Richarius seized the opportunity to give the king all sorts of good advice. Pleased at Richarius's lack of flattery and his frankness, the king gave him a substantial sum of money which Richarius in turn gave to the poor.

~

The most famous advice that Richarius gave Dagobert was this: "He who has to obey will only have to render account to God of himself, but he who commands will also have to answer for all his subjects."

APRIL 27

Zita

(d. 1278)

BORN INTO A POOR TUSCAN FAMILY, Zita possessed a sweet character and disciplined work habits that were put to use as a domestic servant in the house of the Fatinelli family. At first, Zita's attention to her duties and her piety aroused the anger of her fellow workers, but her cheerfulness and kindness won them over. Even as the housekeeper in charge of the rest of the staff, a role which she eventually assumed, Zita attended Mass daily, distributed even her own food to the poor, and often gave up her own bed to the homeless. Zita died at the age of sixty, having served the same family for over forty-eight years.

∼

This story, legendary in many of its aspects, is often told about Zita. One Christmas Eve, when she was leaving the house for Mass, her employer lent her his own fur cloak because of the bitter cold. He made her promise, however, to bring it back. At the door of the church, Zita saw a beggar freezing in thin rags and impulsively gave him the fur cloak. She asked the beggar to return it to her when the service was over. When she exited from the church she found that the beggar and the cloak had disappeared. Zita returned home to her employer's anger. On Christmas day, however, the story came to a happy ending. A stranger came to the door of the Fatinelli house and returned the missing fur.

People later concluded that the beggar must have been an angel in disguise, and so the door of the church where he first appeared is called the "Angel Portal."

APRIL 28

Louis-Marie Grignion de Montfort

(d. 1716)

BORN INTO A POOR FRENCH FAMILY, Louis-Marie was ordained in 1700. He was assigned as a chaplain to a hospital at Poitiers, but his reorganization of the staff at the hospital caused wide resentment. He wrote a popular book entitled True Devotion to the Blessed Virgin, *and founded the Montfort Fathers to spread devotion to Mary.*

~

Here is Louis-Marie's thoughts on spiritual wealth: "Do as the storekeeper does with his merchandise; make a profit on every article. Suffer not the loss of the tiniest fragment of the true cross. It may only be the sting of a fly or a point of a pin that annoys you; it may be the little eccentricities of a neighbor, some unintentional slight, the insignificant loss of a penny, some little restlessness of soul, a slight physical weakness, a light pain in your limbs. Make a profit on every article as the grocer does, and you will soon be wealthy in God."

About suffering he also said: "To suffer much, yet badly, is to suffer like reprobates. To suffer much, even bravely, but for a wicked cause, is to suffer as a martyr of the devil. To suffer much or little for the sake of God is to suffer like the saints."

Catherine of Siena
(d. 1380)

YOUNGEST OF TWENTY-FIVE CHILDREN, Catherine had a twin sister who died at birth. As a child she was so merry that the family gave her the pet name of Euphrosyne, which is a Greek word for "joy." Later, as a teenager, she declared her intention not to marry. To reinforce this choice, she cut off her beautiful hair. Her mother responded to this act by assigning her the most menial household tasks. Her father finally realized that further opposition would only strengthen Catherine's resolve, so he allowed her the use of a small, dark room as a cell. For the next three years, she spoke to no one except her confessor. At nineteen, after a vision of Christ placing a ring on her finger, she returned to normal family life and began to care for the sick, the poor, and the imprisoned. With twenty-three of her companions, she undertook a diplomatic journey to Avignon where the pope had taken up residence. There she entreated the pope to return to Rome which he did. Afterwards, she returned to Siena where she wrote The Dialogue, *her spiritual masterpiece. She died at age thirty-three of a stroke.*

～

Catherine was often subjected to fearsome spiritual trials. She had long intervals of desolation, during which God appeared to have abandoned her completely. She asked, "Oh, Lord, where were you when my heart was so sorely vexed with foul and hateful temptations?" Our Lord answered, "Daughter, I was in your heart fortifying you by my grace."

Piety is not a question of environment as Catherine of Siena pointed out. She wrote William Flete about his refusal to visit her in Rome because he felt he would lose his piety if he left the countryside: "Your piety must not be very solid if you lose it while changing homes. It would seem that God only stays in the forest and not in places where He is most needed."

Catherine was often outspoken but showed great courtesy to whomever she met. However, she called Pope Gregory XI, "my sweet Babbo."

Catherine gave this advice: "Build yourself a cell in your heart and retire there to pray."

APRIL 30
Pius V
(pope) (d. 1572)

A DOMINICAN, Pius V enforced the decrees of the Council of Trent which had ended two years before his election. He supervised revisions of the Roman Missal and the Roman Breviary, published the Roman Catechism, and continued the harsh work of the Inquisition. Pius V brought his monastic sensibilities to the papacy, wearing his white Dominican habit, walking instead of riding, and taking his frugal meals in solitude. He also attempted to sweep the Papal States free of moral abuses, including bullfighting, adultery, prostitution, and blasphemy.

Pius V met death with these words: "Lord, increase my sufferings but increase my patience also."

During his time as a teacher of philosophy and theology, Pius traveled often to Milan to hear the confession of the Marquis of Guast. He never could be persuaded to buy a cloak to defend himself from the rain, saying: "Poor followers of the gospel ought to be content with one tunic." He performed this journey on foot and in strict silence.

May

MAY 1
Peregrine Laziosi
(d. 1345)

AS AN ANTIPAPAL ACTIVIST IN ITALY, Peregrine struck Philip Benizi in the face as Philip was trying to quiet a street demonstration. Peregrine was so startled by Philip's acceptance of the blow and his offering of the other cheek that he had a complete change of heart. He joined the Servite Order, was ordained, and then founded a new Servite house. He became famed for his preaching, austerities, holiness, and ability as a confessor.

Peregrine is invoked against cancer because of the following story: At one point Peregrine became afflicted with cancer of the foot—a condition that was not only extremely painful but one that caused people who saw him to be repelled. Finally, his doctors decided that their only recourse was to amputate Peregrine's foot. The night before the operation Peregrine spent hours in prayer and finally fell asleep. He woke the next morning to find himself completely cured.

Athanasius of Alexandria
(d. 373)

ATHANASIUS WAS A DEACON in Alexandria when he led the battle against Arianism—a heresy that held that Christ was not eternal or co-equal with the Father. Educated at the catechetical school of Alexandria, Athanasius accompanied his bishop to the Council of Nicaea in 325. As the debate over Arianism proceeded, Athanasius saw the seriousness of the situation and helped to form persuasive arguments against the heretics.

In the turbulent times that followed, the Arians mounted political and doctrinal attacks against Athanasius and managed to get him exiled at least five times. In the meantime, Athanasius became a bishop, also taking on the welfare of the desert monks and fathers, as well as those Christians in Ethiopia where the faith had just taken root. During his exiles, Athanasius spent his time in theological writing and always managed to maintain the support of his clergy and people. Athanasius spent the last seven years of his life in Alexandria. An intense man, Athanasius was also known for his not-so-gentle humor, which he used as a weapon in his arsenal to support the Catholic faith.

～

At one point, the Arians had accused Athanasius of the murder of a Meletian bishop, Arsenius, who in fact had not been killed but was in hiding. Athanasius was compelled to appear before a council convened at Tyre in 335 to answer this charge. After his accusers produced a hand that they said Athanasius had cut off the murdered Arsenius, Athanasius is said to have produced the very-much-alive Arsenius in court. First pointing out his face, he then drew out from the bishop's cloak first one, then the other hand, and said, "Let no one now ask for a third, for God has only given a man two hands."

Athanasius had this to say about our eternal fate: "All of us are naturally frightened of dying and the dissolution of our bodies, but remember this most startling fact: that those who accept the faith of the cross despise even what is normally terrifying, and for the sake of Christ cease to fear even death. When He became man, the Savior's love put away death from us and renewed us again; for Christ became man that we might become God."

MAY 3

Philip of Zell

(d. *c*.770)

AN ENGLISH TRAVELER who settled near what is now the city of Worms, Philip was joined in his hermitage by another hermit named Horskolf who helped Philip cultivate the land. Gradually disciples gathered around the two of them, and eventually the monastery of Zell, named after his hermit's cell, was founded.

～

A legendary story is told about this saintly hermit: One evening robbers stole the two oxen which Philip and Horskolf kept in order to help them with the cultivation of their land. All night through the thieves wandered about the area, lost and unable to find their way out. In the morning, they discovered that they were back exactly where they started from, right in front of the hermitage. In fear and distress, they begged forgiveness of Philip. He reassured them, even giving them food and provisions to help them on their journey.

Florian of Austria

(d. 304)

A DISTINGUISHED OFFICER in the Roman army in what is now Austria, Florian had secretly become a Christian. When the emperor Diocletian ordered that all Christian churches and books be burned, Florian decided not to conceal his faith and gave himself up to the Roman authorities. After professing his faith, he was scourged twice, then his skin was slowly peeled from his body. Finally, instead of being executed by the sword and thus given a soldier's death, Florian was thrown into the river Ems with a stone around his neck. Many miracles are attributed to Florian, among them the extinguishing of a huge fire with only a small pitcher of water.

∽

While Florian was being tortured, he rejoiced and said: "Be as angry and do as much harm as you can, since you possess power over my body which has been given to you now. If you want to know why I do not fear your tortures, light a fire, and I will climb upon it to heaven."

John of Beverley

(d. 721)

Born in Yorkshire, England, John studied at Canterbury, became a monk at Whitby Abbey, and was made a bishop, serving eventually at York. He founded a monastary at Beverley to which he retreated periodically for prayer. He died worn out by old age.

∽

John of Beverley is invoked against baldness. A story is told of him that he once took into his retreat a young man who was dumb as well as bald. John made the sign of the cross on the youth's tongue and he miraculously obtained his speech; moreover, he was also cured of his baldness.

Peter's practice of distributing May Bread (free bread and soup) in the weeks before the harvest when food was scarce was continued until the French Revolution.

MAY 10
Isidore the Farmer
(d. 1130)

Patron of farmers, Isidore was a day laborer, working on the farm of the wealthy landowner just outside Madrid, Spain. Isidore's life was a model of charity and prayer. After a day of hard physical labor he still had time to visit the many churches in Madrid. Isidore shared what he had—even his meals—with the poor, often giving them the larger portions.

Because of his popularity, many unsubstantiated stories have grown around Isidore. Here is one: A complaint was made that Isidore arrived late to work because he attended early morning Mass each day. When rebuked by his employer, Isidore explained to his employer: "It may be true that I am later at my work than some of the others, but I do my utmost to make up for the few minutes snatched for prayer; please compare my work with theirs, and if you find I have defrauded you in the least, I will gladly make restitution by paying you out of my own purse."

Still suspicious and determined to find out the truth, his employer rose early one morning and followed Isidore from the church to the field where he was working. The employer saw Isidore take the plow into a field and, in the morning mists, he saw a second plow drawn by white oxen moving up and down the furrows. Astonished, he ran toward this vision, but even as he neared, it disappeared. When he spoke to Isidore about the second plow, Isidore replied in surprise: "Sir, I work alone and know only God to whom I look for strength."

MAY 10
Antoninus of Florence
(d. 1459)

AS A BOY, Antoninus was so frail that his stepmother fed him extra servings of meat. Antoninus, however, determined to harden himself for the religious life, would slip the meat under the table to the cats. Antoninus spent much time begging God for the grace to avoid sin. At the age of fourteen, Antoninus requested entrance to the newly reformed Florence house of the Dominicans. The superior, not wishing to undermine his youthful enthusiasm, told him to go home and memorize a very large book called Decretum Gratiani, *hoping to discourage him. With great determination, however, he spent a year memorizing the book straight through and returned to recite it and be received into the Dominican Order.*

Ordained and set to preaching, Antoninus soon won his place in the hearts of the Florentines. As an influential superior in the Dominican Order, Antoninus zealously enforced reforms that restored the primitive Dominican rule.

Antoninus's became bishop of Florence with great reservations. He was a "people's bishop" and discharged his duties with justice and charity. At Antoninus's death, he was deeply mourned by the whole city of Florence.

∽

When Antoninus's secretary said to him that bishops were to be pitied if they were to be eternally besieged with hurry as he was, the saint answered in this way: "To enjoy interior peace, we must always reserve in our hearts amid all affairs, as it were, a secret closet, where we are to keep retired within ourselves, and where no business of the world can ever enter."

Antoninus's kindness to the poor was legendary. He pulled up his own flower garden and planted vegetables for the poor. He drove his housekeeper to distraction by giving away his own tableware, food, clothing, and furniture. He generally rode around Florence on a mule, which he often sold to help some poor person. When that happened, a wealthy citizen would buy the animal back and offer it as a present to the charitable bishop.

MAY 10
Mary Mazzarello
(d. 1881)

FOUNDER OF THE SALESIAN SISTERS who aimed to do for girls what Don Bosco had done for boys, Mary was born into a peasant family and spent her early years working in the fields. Despite her limited education, Mary was known for her management skills, her gentleness, and her general happiness. She died at the young age of forty-four.

～

Exhibiting humorous coolness when facing death, Saint Mary remarked to the priest who had given her the last rites: "Well, that's the passport. I expect I can leave any time now."

Julian of Norwich

(d. *c*.1423)

AN ENGLISH MYSTIC who lived as a solitary near Norwich, England. Nothing is known of her life before she became an anchorite. In her solitude, she wrote her spiritual masterpiece Revelations of Divine Love. *Julian has never formally been beatified.*

~

Julian's book is full of deep insights. Among them are these:

- Our soul can never have rest in things that are beneath itself.
- God can do all that we need.
- I knew well that while I beheld the cross I was surely safe.
- The greatest honor you can give Almighty God is to live gladly, joyfully because of the knowledge of His love.
- It is true that sin is the cause of all this pain: but all shall be well, and all shall be well, and all manner of things shall be well.
- Peace and love are always alive in us, but we are not always alive to peace and love.

MAY 14

Pachomius of Tabenna

(d. c.346–348)

PACHOMIUS WAS FORCED TO JOIN THE THEBAN ARMY under horrible conditions. As a recruit, he was treated with great kindness by the Christians who came to his aid. This kindness from strangers convinced Pachomius to become a Christian and to enter a monastery. This he did and, after founding a new monastery, Pachomius wrote the first communal rule for monks.

~

Pachomius often said sickness or affliction was for the good for the soul. Saint Theodorus, who after his death succeeded him as superior general, was afflicted with a perpetual headache. Pachomius, when asked by some of the brethren to pray for his health, answered: "Though abstinence and prayer be of great merit, yet sickness, suffered with patience, is of much greater."

Pachomius says this about humility: "It is very much better for you to be one among a crowd of a thousand people and to possess very little humility, than to be a man living in the cave of a hyena in pride."

MAY 19

Celestine V

(pope) (d. 1296)

CELESTINE FOUNDED THE BENEDICTINE CELESTINES and was elected pope at the age of eighty-four after a vote that took two years to complete. Reigning for only five months, he resigned after an uproar resulting from his inability to manage the af-

fairs of the papacy. He fled to the woods and was finally captured, some say hidden, by his successor in a secret room in the Pope's palace. One source says that when Celestine entered his hiding place he said: "Finally a cell....That's all I ever wanted, a cell," and "Oh, the luxury of peace and quiet."

⁓

The eleventh of twelve children, Celestine knew his vocation at a very early age. When his mother would ask of her children, "Which one of you will become a saint when you grow up?" Celestine would quickly reply, "Me, I'll be the saint!"

A story about the two-year conclave tells us that when Celestine sent a note to the cardinals saying that God was not pleased that they were taking so long to decide on a pope, they chose him, a humble hermit, just to keep God happy!

MAY 20

Bernardine of Siena

(d. 1444)

BORN NEAR SIENA, Bernardine gave away all his possessions and joined the Franciscans. Soon after ordination, he embarked on a preaching career that he pursued right up until his death. Bernardine was responsible for spreading the devotion to the Holy Name of Jesus.

⁓

The following story recounts Saint Bernardine's unfortunate attempt to be a hermit: "One day there came to me the idea that I should live on herbs and water, and in order to do this, I thought that I had better go and take up my abode in a wood. Then I started asking myself questions:

'What will you do in a wood? What will you eat?' My reply was: 'I shall do exactly what the holy fathers did. I shall eat herbs when I am hungry and drink water when I am thirsty. It is quite simple.' So I decided to start on my new life. I bought a Bible which I could meditate upon in my wood, and to prevent it from getting wet or soiled, I bought a piece of leather to cover it. My next step was to find a place to roost, so I went as far as the valley of Bochegiano where I climbed, first on the top of one hill, and then on to the top of another to view the land, all the time, saying to myself, as I looked around, 'That seems to be a very nice place—but that over there is a better place.' I got so bewildered I could not decide upon any place, and returned to Siena.

"Still, the idea of a hermit's life would cling to me, so I decided to try again, and one day, I went out as far as Follonica, where I gathered some sowthistles and other nasty herbs with which to make a salad. Such a salad! There was neither salt nor oil, and no bread. However, I reasoned with myself, 'Now, let us start this new life by washing and scraping the salad this first time, and another time we shall not wash it, but simply scrape it, and when we are accustomed to it, we shall not scrape it, so by degrees we shall arrive at such a point that we shall not even gather it.' When I began to chew, it remained solid in my mouth, it would not go down. Shall I tell you something? One mouthful of sowthistles took away from me every temptation to lead that kind of life.'"

This comment was given by Bernardine to a spouse who had high standards for his wife: "How would you like this wife of yours to be? You reply, "I want her not to be greedy." But you are always at your food. You say, "I'd like her to be active." And yet you are a proper sluggard. You continue,

"I'd like her peaceful." And you would burst into a rage at a straw if it crossed your feet. She must be "Obedient." And yet you obey neither father, nor mother, nor anyone. You don't deserve a woman like her. You sum it up, "I want a wife who is good and attractive and wise and well brought up." My answer is that if you want her to be like this, then you must be that way too.

MAY 21
Eugene de Mazenod
(d. 1861)

PATRON OF DYSFUNCTIONAL FAMILIES, Eugene grew up in a situation of family conflict. Though French by birth, his family fled to Italy when he was a young boy to escape the French Revolution. Afterwards his parents divorced, his mother returning to France, his father remaining in Italy. Torn apart by the split-up of his family and the pull of religious life, he began teaching catechism and finally entered the seminary at the age of twenty-six and was ordained three years later. Eugene chose the life of a parish priest, working among the poor, the sick, and the marginalized. Because of this work, he founded the Oblates of Mary Immaculate and was appointed bishop of Marseilles in 1837. In all, he founded twenty-three parishes, either built or rebuilt some fifty churches, restored discipline in the clergy, developed catechisms for the youth, cared for the retired priests, and was personally responsible for doubling the number of priests in his diocese. His writings fill some twenty-five volumes.

~

Some of his words of wisdom include:

- "I am a priest for Christ...that sums it all up, nothing more need be said!"

- "If you love the Church, you love Christ, and vice versa."
- "Leave no stone unturned in your quest for God's eternal kingdom."
- "I am happiest in missionary and pastoral work... not to pay court to the great or waste my time amongst the rich. That's not the way to become a cardinal...but if a person could become a saint, wouldn't that be even better?"
- "How should you conduct yourself if you want to follow in the footsteps of Jesus? You must strive to be saints...walk their same paths, renounce yourself completely, strive only for God's glory, the good of the Church, and the salvation of souls."
- "We are all children of God...servants, farm workers, peasants, the poor, the diseased, suffering...you are all co-heirs to the Kingdom. In you is an immortal soul that was made in God's image...you are more precious in God's eyes than all the riches on earth. Know that dignity!"

MAY 22

Rita of Cascia
(d. 1457)

IN SPITE OF THE PIETY OF HER PARENTS and her desire to enter a convent, Rita was promised in marriage to an abusive, promiscuous man. Obedient to her parents, she married him and soon became the mother of twin boys. Enduring his various abuses for eighteen years, she was widowed when her husband was killed in a vendetta. She dissuaded her sons from avenging their father's death; however they, too, soon died. Applying to the Augustinians for admittance, she was refused three times (they would only accept virgins) before they made an exception. In response to her prayers asking to share in Christ's suffering, she received a wound on her head (as if she was wearing a crown of thorns) that lasted for fifteen years.

～

The roses that are blessed in some churches on Rita's feast day arise from this story: When Rita was near death, she asked a visitor to go back to the garden of her birthplace to bring her a rose and two figs. It was far to early for roses and fruit to bloom but the visitor complied with her request. The visitor returned to the garden and, to her great surprise, she found a rosebush in full bloom and two ripe figs on a leafless tree.

MAY 23
Bartholomew Pucci
(d. 1330)

A LAYMAN, BARTHOLOMEW renounced his wife, children, and social position to take the rough habit of the Franciscans, making sure to provide for the welfare of his wife and children. His wife also consecrated herself to God. Bartholomew's love for Christ was so strong that he never refused a favor from anyone who asked it in God's name.

～

Bartholomew is one of the saints who are called "fools for Christ." He went about the streets doing things to make people laugh at him and make them think that he had lost his mind.

Madeleine Sophie Barat
(d. 1865)

BORN IN FRANCE, she was educated by her older brother who later became a priest. While still a very young woman, she founded the Society of the Sacred Heart of Jesus, a religious institute for the education of girls. By the time of her death, she had opened more than one hundred houses and schools in twelve countries.

~

Madeleine would often say: "If the world knew our happiness [as members of the Society of the Sacred Heart], it would, out of sheer envy, invade our retreats, and the times of the fathers of the Desert would return when the solitudes were more populous than the cities." She would often advise: "Too much work is a danger for an imperfect soul...but for one who loves our Lord...it is an abundant harvest."

Philip Neri
(d. 1595)

PHILIP WAS A ROMAN PRIEST who devoted himself to the study of theology as well as to serving his neighbors, notably the youth, the ill, and prisoners. He founded a company of priests, the Congregation of the Oratory of Divine Love, whose goals are prayer, preaching, and parish ministry. The German poet, Goethe, called him "The Humorous Saint" and his room had a sign at the door: "The House of Christian Mirth." He was a man of various emotions, happy, sad, empathetic, pious, but mainly pious. It is said that he was "all things to all men...when he was called upon to be merry, he was; if there was a demand upon his sympathy, he was equally ready for that." He was much sought after, people came from all over just to speak with him.

~

On the feast day of Corpus Christi (May 25, 1595), he was in a radiantly happy mood. Many, including his personal physician, told him that he hadn't looked to be in better health in ten years. He had been hearing confessions with unusual zeal the entire day, for he knew his end was near. Upon retiring, he said, "Last of all, we must die." And he did, shortly after midnight.

Philip Neri once prescribed a "simple mortification" to a hopeless drunkard. "Drink all the wine you want," the saint told him cheerfully, "just no water." The drunk was cured in a week, because all know that there's nothing like alcohol to make a person thirsty.

This is also an oft-told story about Philip Neri: One day, Philip said to one of his penitents, "In penance, young lady, you will pluck a chicken while walking in the street. After that, you will turn around and backtrack and pick up all the fallen feathers."

"All the feathers?" replied the girl. "But that is impossible, Father!"

"Well," pointed out Philip, "it is also as impossible to take back all the damaging effects your gossip has spread throughout the city."

Philip's humor was always tinged with reality: Once a young priest once asked Saint Philip Neri what prayer would be best to say after a wedding ceremony and nuptial Mass. He lightheartedly replied: "A prayer for peace."

A few other words of wisdom include the following:

- "A glad spirit attains perfection more quickly than any other."
- "I will have no sadness in my house."
- "Christian joy is a gift of God flowing from a good conscience."
- "Cheerfulness strengthens the heart and makes us try harder to have a good life, thus God's servants must always be in good spirits."
- "A heart filled with joy is more easily made perfect than one that is sad."

MAY 27
Augustine of Canterbury
(d. 605)

BORN IN ROME, Augustine became a monk and was sent to the British Isles. He is the person largely responsible for the spread of Christianity throughout England. He was the first archbishop of Canterbury and established episcopal sees at London and Rochester.

~

About the great generosity of God, Augustine said: "In His promises to hear our prayers, God wants to come to us...ask if you need anything and He will give you something better than you'll ever imagine."

With reference to the spiritual life, he said: "He who must climb to a lofty height [of holiness], must do so by baby steps, not giant leaps!"

MAY 29

Richard Thirkeld

(d. 1583)

OXFORD EDUCATED, *he entered the priesthood later in life, studying in France. Returning home to England (York), he was arrested for the crime of being a priest. Two months later he was convicted and, one day later, was hanged, drawn, and quartered.*

~

On the day he was condemned to death, he fell on his knees, saying "This is the day the Lord has made. Let us be glad and rejoice." Richard's court record says that the prosecutor ordered him martyred in secret so that he "wouldn't become one of those bothersome martyred saints from that Church in Rome."

MAY 30

Joan of Arc

(d. 1431)

JOAN WAS ONE OF FIVE CHILDREN *born to a well-respected farmer. Her visions and mystical experiences led her to search for the "true king" of France and help him reclaim his throne. Disguised, she led troops in battle, the victories of which brought the throne to Charles VII. Captured and sold to the English for a reported ten thousand francs, she was convicted as a heretic by an ecclesiastical court and burned at the stake in Rouen. In 1456, at the request of her mother and two brothers, her trial was reopened and she was acquitted (twenty-three years later). Various reports attest to the fact that each of her accusers and executioners met with untimely and violent ends.*

Joan was reported to have said these things during her trial:

- "About Jesus and the Church, I know just one simple thing, we shouldn't complicate the matter!"
- "I trust completely in God, nothing else."
- "Help yourself and God will help you."

Joan abhorred swearing and coined the following phrase: "By my martin" which she used to express her anger and dismay.

June

JUNE 1
Justin Martyr
(d. 165)

IMPRESSED BY THE HEROISM and faith of the Christian martyrs, Justin became a Christian at the age of thirty. An influential and learned speaker, he used these skills to effect many conversions. Greatly displeased by Justin's success, the Roman prefect ordered Justin beheaded because of his beliefs and refusal to revert to paganism. He is recognized as one of the first to stress the designation of the color white as an indication of purity: "If your sins are scarlet, as Isaiah tells us, through faith, they will become white as the wool of a sheep; if they are just crimson, they will become like the white of snow."

Justin wrote to demonstrate the superiority of Christianity over paganism, pointing out that practical benefit to society alone recommended it: "We who formerly delighted in fornication now cleave only to chastity. We who exercised the magic arts now consecrate ourselves to the good and unbegotten God. We who valued above all else the acquisition of wealth and property now direct all that we have to a common fund, which is shared with every needy person. We who hated and killed one another, and who, because of differing customs, would not share a fireside with those of another race, now, after the appearance of Christ, live together with them. We pray for our enemies, and try to persuade those who unjustly hate us that, if they live according to the excellent precepts of Christ, they will have a good hope of receiving the same reward as ourselves, from the God Who governs all."

JUNE 3

John XXIII

(pope) (d. 1963)

BORN IN BERGAMO, ITALY, in 1881, John was ordained in 1904 and served in Vatican diplomatic posts before being made a cardinal. Following the death of Pope Pius XII, he was elected pope at the age of seventy-seven. John's major contribution of his short pontificate was the calling of the Second Vatican Council. He did not live to see its completion.

A new building was being constructed on the Vatican grounds. The architect submitted his plans to Pope John XXIII, who, shortly afterward, returned them with these three Latin words written in the margin: "*Non sumus angeli,*" which means "We are not angels." The architect and his staff couldn't figure out what the pope meant, until, finally, someone noticed that the plans did not include bathrooms.

The first time Pope John XXIII was carried on the papal throne, he asked, "How much did Pacelli [predecessor as pope and very slight in build] weigh?"

Without waiting for an answer, he added, "From now on, your salary is doubled."

When asked by a reporter how many people work in the Vatican, Pope John XXIII answered good-naturedly, "About half of them!"

Always kind and gentle, Pope John XXIII never changed, even when he was elevated to the highest office of his Church. When his own family, the Roncalli brothers and sisters, entered the papal palace for their first visit, they knelt, shy and awkward, before the papal throne. The pontiff extended his hands, smiled, and said, "Don't be afraid, it's only me."

JUNE 4

Petroc
(d. 594)

AFTER STUDYING IN IRELAND, Petroc returned to Britain where he lived a monk's life in a monastery which he founded. After thirty years, Petroc went on a pilgrimage to Rome and, upon his return, retreated even more deeply into the forest to live in solitude.

~

As one of the saints of the Dark Ages in Cornwall, many folktales and stories are intertwined in the person of Petroc. Here are the most familiar: One day it began to rain, and Petroc predicted it would stop, but it continued to storm for three long days. In penance for presuming to predict God's weather, Petroc exiled himself to an island off the coast of India, where he remained for seven years. During his sojourn there, legend tells us that he made friends with a wolf, which he brought back to England and used to defeat a mighty serpent that the king had sent to destroy him and his followers.

Boniface

(d. 754)

A BRITISH MONK AND MISSIONARY to Germany, Boniface was eventually appointed the archbishop of Mainz. Boniface built religious houses all over Germany as well as evangelizing Holland where he was martyred with fifty of his followers.

~

On one occasion, Boniface encountered a tribe who worshiped a God in the form of a huge oak tree. Legend relates that Boniface walked up to the tree, removed his shirt, grabbed an axe and hacked it down. As the tree fell, Boniface said: "See how weak your god is? Mine is mightier than the axe!" The pagans immediately converted. With their help, he built a church on the site with the wood from the oak tree.

Boniface had this to say: "The Church, in her voyage across the oceans of earth, is like a great ship that is being assailed by the waves caused by the stresses in life. As Christians, our duty is to not abandon ship and keep her on her chosen course."

Jarlath

(d. 540)

AN IRISH NOBLE, Jarlath became a priest and founded a monastery and school in County Galway. He was known as a great teacher and so his school attracted scholars from all over Ireland; two of his better-known students include Saint Brendan and Saint Colman of Cloyne. His feast is celebrated through-out Ireland.

~

Saint Jarlath is reputed to have prayed, on his knees, three hundred times during the day and three hundred times during the night. It is said that he prayed so much that he could never straighten his legs completely.

JUNE 8

Medard

(d. 558)

BORN TO A NOBLE FRENCH FAMILY, ordained at the age of thirty-three, Medard was a notable preacher and missionary.

~

As a great favorite in rural France, Medard is the subject of many popular stories. When he was a child, Medard was once sheltered from a severe rainstorm by the wings of an eagle. From this event comes the belief that if it rains on his feast day, the next forty days will also have rain, and if the weather is good, it will remain fair for the next forty days as well. He is the patron saint of good weather. He is also known as the patron of those with a toothache because it is written that when he laughed, which was frequently, he did so with his mouth wide open, displaying his incredibly beautiful teeth. He is an early proponent of the theory that laughter is the best medicine (he lived to the ripe old age of ninety)!

Columba

(d. 597)

MIRACLE WORKER, PRIEST, AND TEACHER, Columba founded numerous monasteries throughout Ireland. Columba was exiled to the island of Iona because of his complicity in a feud that eventually led to the deaths of three thousand people. From Iona, Columba evangelized large parts of Scotland.

Columba dearly loved manuscripts and was always desirous of obtaining them from whatever the source. Columba's former teacher, Finnian, had obtained the first copy of Jerome's psalter to reach Ireland. Columba "borrowed" the book and secretly made a copy of his own. When Finnian found out what had happened, he claimed the copied manuscript and referred his claim to King Diarmaid of Ireland. The decision went against Columba. Said the judge: "To every cow her calf, and to every book its son-book."

The description of Columba left by his biographer says this about him: "He had the face of an angel: he was of an excellent nature, polished in speech, holy in deed, great in counsel...And, in the midst of all his toils, he appeared loving unto all, serene and holy, rejoicing in the joy of the Holy Spirit in his inmost heart."

John Maximovitch of Tobolsk

(d. 1715)

THOUGH A MEMBER of the Russian nobility, John was a religious child who later became a monk and teacher at Kievan College. For the next twenty years, Father John led various monasteries in southern Russia: an inspiration to all by virtue of his piety and penance. He was a prolific writer.

~

On the day of his death (he had been made aware of its approach), he celebrated the Divine Liturgy, and held a dinner in his home, serving the dignitaries himself as outlined in the Gospel (see Luke 14:13–14). Bidding farewell to his clergy, he closed himself up in his quarters. He was later discovered to have died when he failed to answer the community's vesper bells.

John's most important work, *Ilotropian*, took a number of years to complete. The title is the Greek word for sunflower, an image dear to the saint, even from his youth, an image he used to explain the agreement of our will to that of God's. The sunflower has the unique trait of following the movements of the sun with its facelike flower. A common sight in his homeland, this image was one to which his followers could relate: "The only true means for happiness in this life as well as the next is to turn our wills, deeds, actions in entire devotion to God, just as does the sunflower as she follows the sun's path across the sky….As the sunflower grows, so does our faith…if we follow the one true Sun." And further: "Even on cloudy days, the sunflower is vigilant, unchanging in its love….Our sun is God's will; it does not always illuminate our path without clouds....We may have clear days followed by cloudy ones...but may our love for God be so strong that we are inseparable, even in sorrow and misfortune."

Barnabas

(first century)

ALTHOUGH HE WAS NOT CHOSEN as one of the original twelve apostles, he is treated as an apostle by the early Church Fathers. He was selected by the apostles to spread the Gospel to Antioch and lead the new converts. Later, captured by certain Jews, he was burned to death.

~

Originally named Joseph, the apostles changed his name to Barnabas, which means "a man of encouragement" or "the son of consolation." Barnabas's good-hearted acceptance of Gentiles and of Paul is described in Acts 26–29. As Mr. Encouragement, Barnabas was sent to Antioch, and when he arrived he saw the grace of God among the believers and rejoiced (Acts 11:22–26).

JUNE 13

Anthony of Padua

(d. 1231)

SON OF A CAPTAIN in the Spanish army, Anthony was born in Lisbon and at first entered the Augustinian Order. When a fellow brother brought stories of the glorious martyrdom of Franciscans in Morocco, Anthony became determined to enter this order. He quickly left on an expedition to convert the Is-lamics of Morocco, but he fell ill and had to return to Sicily where he was offered shelter by the Franciscans. Recovering, he was sent to a quiet Franciscan monastery where he remained for nine months as the chaplain to the monks, meditating and performing menial duties.

Anthony was appointed to fill in for a priest who was to give the sermon on the occasion of an ordination. He startled all present by his eloquence and knowledge. Immediately, his assignment was altered and he was given the mission to preach throughout Italy. It is said that he was such a convincing preacher that even heretics returned to the Church after hear-ing one of his sermons.

~

Some of his Anthony's jewels of wisdom include the fol-lowing:

- "Consider every day as a new beginning, the first day of your life; and always act with the same fer-vor."
- "Actions speak louder than words; let your words teach and your actions speak….It is useless for a person to flaunt the law if their actions undermine it."
- "The saints are like stars….Christ conceals them in a hidden place so that they might not shine be-fore their time…but they are always there, ready to do so."
- "Happy is the man whose words come from the Holy Spirit and not himself."

Germaine Cousin

(d. 1601)

BORN NEAR TOULOUSE, FRANCE, *Germain suffered from a form of tuberculosis and a deformed hand. Losing her mother as an infant, Germaine was ignored by her father and abused by her stepmother who sentenced Germaine to sleep in a cupboard under the stairs or in the barn, and who allowed her to eat only scraps and garbage. She also administered beatings and scaldings with boiling water. In spite of being banished to field work, Germaine refused to miss Mass. Each time she heard the church bells, she would lay her staff on the ground, send a prayer to her guardian angel to watch over her sheep and then, in a complete state of trust, walk to the church. Nothing ever harmed her animals while she was at Mass, even though the nearby woods were filled with wolves. In spite of her poverty, Germaine shared whatever meager food she had with others who were poorer than herself. Shortly before her death, her family recognized her goodness and decided to treat her well. But Germain opted to stay where she was. One morning, in 1601, Germaine's father went to awaken her and found her dead on her pallet of straw and twigs. She was just twenty-two years old.*

~

Once, during a hard winter, her stepmother accused Germaine of stealing bread to feed a beggar, threatening her with yet another beating. Demanding that Germain open the folds of her apron, which she did, she was astounded to see the most glorious summer flowers fall from it. Expressing her extraordinary powers of forgiveness, Germaine took one of the flowers and presented it to her stepmother saying: "Please accept this flower. God sends it to you as a sign of his forgiveness."

Her prayers were simple, yet heartfelt. One includes the following: "Dear God, please don't let me get too hungry or too thirsty, for I need my strength to do your work."

JUNE 19

Romuald
(d. 1027)

BORN INTO ITALIAN NOBILITY, Romuald was a "wild child" who sought to atone for his profligate life by becoming a monk. He founded many monasteries and hermitages throughout Italy and Germany. Some years later, his father, so impressed by his son's metamorphosis, also entered a monastery near Ravenna. Romuald died at the age of seventy.

～

The locals launched a plot to assassinate Romuald so that they could keep his body (which they considered miraculous) as a means of protection. Hearing of this plan, Romuald feigned madness, immediately falling into disfavor with the locals who subsequently ran him out of town.

Romuald, later in life, was taken to weeping for long period of time. But he did have a certain piece of advice to offer in this regard: "Don't weep too much, for it endangers your sight and makes your head soggy."

Instead of slowing down in his old age, he increased his austerities. It is said that he wore no less than three hair shirts at a time. He ate food with absolutely no seasoning. If any was presented to him (which he detected by sniffing each dish extensively), he would say, "Oh gluttony, gluttony, you will never taste any of this, I declare perpetual war against you."

Aloysius Gonzaga
(d. 1591)

ALOYSIUS'S FATHER WANTED HIM TO BECOME A SOLDIER so, as a young boy of four, Aloysius played with toy guns and, a year later, he took Aloysius with him to a military training camp. At the age of nine, however, he had a spiritual conversion and committed himself to a serious program of penance. Following the wishes of his father, Aloysius appeared often at the royal courts in Italy, but never curtailed his devotions. After transferring his title to his brother, in 1585 he became a Jesuit seminarian. He was so fervent that he had to be forbidden to pray or meditate except at designated times. The aftermath of the plague of 1592 struck him down, and he died at the age of twenty-three. Robert Bellarmine, who was Aloysius's confessor, was of the opinion that Gonzaga had never committed a mortal sin.

~

Though perfectly suited by birth to court life, Aloysius saw it as filled with fraud, poison, and lust. Perhaps in response to this, Aloysius said: "We have no right to pride ourselves on our birth; the great are dust like the poor; perhaps their dust stinks even worse."

On his deathbed, Aloysius kept taking off his headcap. He finally explained to his attendants, as he looked on the crucifix, "He [Jesus] didn't have one on when he died."

Thomas More
(d. 1535)

A NATIVE OF LONDON, More was a lawyer who rose to the position of Lord Chancellor under Henry VIII. He disagreed with Henry over Henry's divorce, resigned his chancellorship, and refused to take the oath of allegiance to Henry as head of the Church. Thomas was imprisoned in the Tower of London for fifteen months after which he was beheaded.

~

Thomas More was good-humored, forgiving, and witty to the very end of his life, even when he was being led to the scaffold. As he walked to his beheading, he told the headsman: "I pray thee, see me safely up, and for my coming down, let me shift for myself."

Thomas wrote, in his last letter to his daughter while awaiting execution in the Tower of London: "Farewell my dear child and pray for me, and I shall for you and all your friends that we may merrily meet in heaven."

Here is his wise observation about power: "Men desire authority for its own sake that they may bear a rule, command and control other men, and live uncommanded and uncontrolled themselves."

Here is Thomas's prescription for the golden mean: "When we feel us too bold, remember our own feebleness. When we feel us too faint, remember Christ's strength."

JUNE 22

Joseph Cafasso

(d. 1860)

JOSEPH CAFASSO LECTURED in moral theology and was a popular teacher, making a deep impression on his young students. He met Don Bosco in 1827, and the two became close friends. It was through Joseph's encouragement that Don Bosco decided that his vocation was working with boys.

~

Some words of wisdom accredited to Joseph include:

- "A few acts of confidence and love are worth more than a thousand 'who knows? who knows?'"
- "Heaven is filled with converted sinners of all kinds and there is room for more."
- "Jesus Christ, in his infinite wisdom, used the words and idioms that were in use among those whom he addressed. You should do likewise."

JUNE 23

Etheldreda

(d. 679)

AN ANGLO-SAXON PRINCESS, Etheldreda was also known as Audrey. She married twice for the sake of family connections, but neither marriage was ever consummated. Her second husband, after a time, weary of this arrangement, tried to bribe the local bishop to release Audrey from her perpetual vow of virginity. The bishop refused. Audrey's husband eventually gave up, the marriage was annulled, and Audrey took formal vows as a religious. She founded the abbey at Ely and died of a large, ugly tumor on her neck which she viewed as divine retribution for all the necklaces she had worn as a vain young woman.

~

In the Middle Ages, a festival was held at Ely on her feast day. It was called Saint Audrey's Fair. It is said to be one of the first religious feast day celebrations in which merchandise was sold to commemorate the event and the saint. Unfortunately, the products sold were of low quality, especially the necklaces. The word "tawdry" was coined as a descriptive adjective, it is believed to be a corruption of "Saint Audrey."

JUNE 24
Bartholomew of Farne
(d. 1193)

ORDAINED A PRIEST IN NORWAY, *Bartholomew returned home, took the monastic habit, and lived the rest of his life as a hermit on Farne Island.*

~

A story tells us that one day, when a mother duck was walking her new ducklings along a cliff one fell into a crevice. The mother hastened to go to Bartholomew and, gifted with a human sense of reason and communication skills, gestured and tugged at the hem of his habit to get him to follow her so he could save her offspring. At once he arose and followed her. Arriving at the place, she pointed at the site of the fall, gazing at her human helper. Approaching the crevice, Bartholomew saw the situation, climbed down and retrieved the duckling. So delighted was the mother that she and her ducklings did a jig and continued on their way. It is said that Bartholomew never lacked eggs for food from that time on, winter or summer.

Cyril of Alexandria

(d. 444)

PATRIARCH OF ALEXANDRIA, *Cyril is named "Doctor of the Incarnation" as well as the "Seal of the Fathers" in the Eastern Church. It is said that he was severe and authoritarian in his practices, and would not adopt any doctrine that had not been learned from the ancient fathers. In a famous conflict with Nestorius, who taught that there were two distinct persons in Christ: God and man, and that Mary couldn't possibly be the mother of Jesus since she was human and he was divine, Cyril sent him into exile. Subsequently, in his writings Cyril insisted on two essential facts about Jesus: that Jesus was begotten by God the Father; and that Jesus was begotten into the flesh of the Blessed Virgin Mary. He is accepted as a brilliant theologian whose writings are characterized by clear thinking, precise explanations, and great reasoning.*

~

Here is an example: "By nature, each of us has our own personality, but supernaturally, we are all united. We are created as one body in Christ because we are nourished by one flesh. Just as Christ is indivisible, we are all united and one in him. That is why he asked the Father: that they may all be one, as we are all one."

"Just the idea that anyone could doubt the right of the Blessed Virgin Mary to be called the Mother of God fills me with astonishment!…that truth has been verified and taught to us by our Holy Fathers."

"The Scriptures affirm that the Word was made flesh."

Irenaeus of Lyons

(d. 202)

THE WRITINGS OF IRENAEUS LAID THE FOUNDATIONS for Christian theology. They emphasize the importance of both the Old and New Testaments, the unity of the gospels, and the true humanity of Jesus within his divinity. Irenaeus was a disciple of Saint Polycarp who had known the apostles. Irenaeus moved to Gaul and became bishop of Lyons where he wrote and spoke against the Gnostic heresy. Irenaeus was convinced that the veil of mystery that enveloped Gnosticism was part of its attraction, and he was determined to "strip the fox," as he expressed it.

∼

Irenaeus writes of the Church and the apostles in these words: "Seeing, therefore, that we have such testimony, we do not need to seek elsewhere the truth which it is easy to find in the Church. For the apostles, like a rich man at a bank, deposited lavishly with her all aspects of the truth, so that everyone, whoever will, may draw from her the water of life. For she is the door to life, and all others are thieves and robbers."

Philip Powell
(d. 1646)

BENEDICTINE MARTYRED UNDER CHARLES I, Philip studied law in London under the future monk and spiritual author, Augustine Baker. When he went to France on business, he became attracted to the Benedictines, and joined their ranks. Sent on the English missions, he worked in Devon, Somerset, and Cornwall for twenty years.

~

Philip conduced a determined defense when he was brought to trial, but when the guilty verdict was given he gave thanks to God in front of the whole court. When an official came to announce the date of his execution, Philip called for a glass of wine with which to drink his health: "Oh, what am I that God honors me and will have me die for his sake?" On the scaffold, just before his hanging, he declared that this was the happiest day of his life.

July

JULY 1

Junipero Serra

(d. 1784)

THE NAMESAKE OF THE SERRA CLUB, an international organization dedicated to promoting vocations, Junipero was a tireless worker who was, in great part, responsible for the spread of the Catholic Church in the western United States. A dedicated Franciscan, he founded twenty-one missions in California. Junipero was even-tempered, kindly in speech, humble, and quiet, picking no quarrels and making no enemies.

This story is recorded by Junipero's biographer: Father Serra and a group of missionaries were on their way back home. The sun was about to set and they had no place to spend the night. Suddenly they saw a poor house near the road, where they went and asked for lodging. There they found an old man, with his wife and child, who received them with much kindness and gave them supper. In the morning, the Fathers thanked their hosts, and went on their way. After having gone a little way they met some other travelers, who asked them where they had spent the night. When the place was described, the travelers declared that there was no such house within miles. The missionaries thought that divine providence was responsible for their hospitality, and believed that their hosts were Jesus, Mary, and Joseph, not only because of the order and cleanliness of the house, and the affectionate kindness of their hosts, with which they had been received, but also because of the extraordinary internal consolation that their hearts had felt there.

JULY 4

Elizabeth of Portugal

(d. 1336)

NAMED FOR HER GREAT-AUNT, Elizabeth of Hungary, Elizabeth of Portugal is also known in Spain as Isabella. Married to the selfish, unfaithful, but effective King Denis, she bore him two children. Although incensed by her husband's debauchery and unfaithfulness, she provided schooling and housing for his numerous illegitimate children.

〜

Elizabeth was known to all as a gifted arbitrator and was credited with having stopped, or prevented, many wars—she was affectionately known as "Elizabeth the Peacemaker." It is reported that her favorite phrase was: "If you love peace, all will be well."

JULY 4

Peter of Luxemburg

(d. 1387)

THOUGH HE DIED AT THE AGE OF EIGHTEEN, Peter was appointed bishop at the age of fourteen and cardinal at the age of sixteen, according to the custom of the time.

〜

Everything about Peter spoke of his charity to the poor. He often said: "Contempt of the world, contempt of yourself: rejoice in your own contempt, but despise no other person."

JULY 6

Sisoes

(d. 429)

EGYPTIAN BY BIRTH, he retired to the desert in search of a more quiet hermitage. Subjecting himself to the austerity of penance, rigors of silence and ardor of continuous prayer, his reputation as a just confessor spread far and wide.

∾

This story is told about Sisoes: A solitary came, time after time, to have his confession heard by Sisoes. He continually confessed to having relapsed in his faith. Sisoes always told him the same thing: "Get up after your fall, go on with your life, don't be discouraged." After a number of the same responses, the man said: "My Father, is there no end to this? How often am I to be told to get up after I fall and get on with my life?" Sisoes replied: "Forever, until death catches up with you and you are either unable or struggling to get up."

JULY 7

Benedict XI

(pope) (d. 1304)

A DOMINICAN, Benedict was a natural diplomat, settling conflicts in Flanders and other places. Elected pope, it is said that the majority of his pontificate was spent undoing the damage done by King Philip of France. A short reign, it was known for leniency and forgiveness.

~

Once, Benedict's mother came to see him in the papal palace. His assistants decided that she was too poorly dressed to be seen in the presence of the pope, so they took her away and dressed her in regal garments. Benedict, recognizing what they had done, said that he did not recognize this affluent woman standing before him in court, asking: "Where is that little widow who came to see me—you know the one I mean? The one who was very pious but poorly dressed—the woman I have loved so much, right from the time of my birth?" The attendants were made to rethink their judgments of the pope's visitors and again were reminded of the equality of all under God's gaze.

JULY 8

Procopius

(d. 303)

AN ASCETIC AND THE FIRST MARTYR OF PALESTINE, Procopius was sentenced to be beheaded for being a Christian. As the executioner lifted the axe, his hands and arms were suddenly paralyzed. Shortly afterwards, his executioner died. Procopius was then taken back to prison and tortured cruelly. Three days later, he was again asked to renounce Christianity and was also charged with witchcraft for the death of his executioner. Before his death, all of Procopius's wounds from his tortures were miraculously healed.

~

The last words on his lips of Procopius were these from Homer: "It is not good to have several masters; let there be one chief, one king."

JULY 9

Veronica Giuliani
(d. 1727)

CAPUCHIN ABBESS IN ITALY, *novice mistress for thirty-four years, and a mystic who also had the stigmata, Veronica had a practical bent: she improved the water supply for the monastery by having it piped in and never let her own mystical experiences interfere with her sensible instruction to her novices.*

~

When Veronica received the stigmata, few believed they were genuine, so her bishop devised a "fraud detecting" plan. The wounds were bandaged and then sealed using his bishop's seal. Put into an area that was separated from her sisters, she was watched around the clock, and she had no communication with the outside world. These requirements made no difference at all and so the bishop allowed her to return to a regular routine.

When she died, her body was examined by the authorities who found that her heart bore the imprint of a cross, a crown of thorns, and a chalice; and her right shoulder was curved as if she had carried a heavy burden—a cross perhaps?

Theodosius

(d. 1074)

THOUGH HE CAME OF A WEALTHY FAMILY, Theodosius dressed like the peasants and worked with them in the fields. He joined the monks of the Caves, Russia's most famous monastery, eventually becoming its abbot. He fostered corporal and spiritual works of mercy, built a hospital, sent food to prisons, and for two years fed and nursed an invalid monk. Theodosius delivered sermons that became a part of Russia's spiritual heritage.

~

Here are some of his best-remembered sayings:

- When listening to the minstrels in the hall of the king, he said: "Sir, will it sound the same in the life to come?"
- "If God's grace does not uphold and nourish us through the poor, what should we do with all our works?"
- "I could not let a day pass without throwing myself in tears at your feet and imploring you not to neglect a single hour of prayer."
- "The young must love their fellows and learn humbly and obediently from their elders; the old must love and help and teach the young, nor must any man make public his mortifications."

Benedict of Nursia

(d. 543)

BORN IN ITALY, Benedict became a hermit and moved to a mountain cave to study the Scriptures. This devotion would continue for the remainder of his life. In spite of his desire to be alone, he acquired disciples from all walks of life. In 527, he traveled to Monte Cassino and established the most famous of his monasteries which became the home of the Benedictine Order. Also at Monte Cassino, he established his famous Rule which revolutionized monastic life in Europe. According to him, a monk was to be a "soldier for God...always on duty." His order was to be a strong family, revering God and the moral value of manual labor.

~

Here are some examples from Benedict's Rule:

- "Concerning the most wretched way of living of all such monks it is better to be silent than to speak."
- "Let the abbot have equal charity for all: let the same discipline be administered in all cases according to merit."
- "When monks rise for the service of God, they shall exhort each other mutually with moderation on account of the excuses that those who are sleepy are inclined to make."
- "Wine can make even the wise go astray."
- "Idleness is the enemy of the soul."
- "The abbot shall order all things in such a way that the strong have something to strive after and the weak nothing at which to take alarm."

JULY 13
Francis Solano
(d. 1610)

A NATIVE OF ANDALUSIA IN SPAIN, Francis became a Franciscan. After twenty years of ministry in Spain, Francis sailed to Peru. He worked there and in other places in South America for the next twenty years. He was said to be able to learn the difficult language of the native peoples in an extraordinarily short time and was understood wherever he went.

～

Music and song were one of Francis's instruments of evangelization. He often cheered the sick with music, played the lute in front of the statue of the Blessed Virgin, and was once seen sitting under a tree, playing his beloved violin, with birds flocking about him and singing along.

JULY 14
Camillus de Lellis
(d. 1614)

BORN OF A MOTHER WHO WAS ALMOST SIXTY at the time of his birth, Camillus was a six-and-a-half foot giant by the time he was seventeen. He joined the army but was dismissed because of an ulcer on his leg. He tried to become a Capuchin and a Franciscan but his ulcerous leg continued to be an impediment. He then became a hospital superintendent and entered the priesthood. He founded the Camillians to serve the sick, including the plague-stricken. Camillus revolutionized nursing, insisting on cleanliness, fresh air, good food, isolation of patients who were contagious, and spiritual help for the dying.

～

To Camillus, serving the sick was serving God—charity was man's life blood. Traveling on foot in all four seasons, impervious to the weather, he said: "The sun is one of God's creatures…it will do me no harm." During his lifetime, he was never sunburned.

Once, a cardinal asked to see Camillus when he was busily tending to the sick. Camillus said: "Tell his excellency to excuse me for, at this moment, I am with Christ, I will see his excellency when I am finished."

When the administration was slow in granting him much-needed supplies, Camillus would go out and beg in the community, saying: "In the whole world, you cannot find a field of flowers that smells sweeter than my hospitals…my holy places." He would always receive what he needed.

JULY 15

Bonaventure

(d. 1274)

REPORTEDLY, THE GREATEST SUCCESSOR of Saint Francis of Assisi, he was to become known as the Seraphic Doctor. One of the greatest scholars in the Church, he is also a Doctor of the Church.

~

Bonaventure was not one to get too excited about honors which people wanted to bestow upon him. Once, a messenger was trudging up the road through the mud to tell him that he had just been appointed cardinal of a large diocese. The messenger was carrying with him the red hat in order to present it to the future cardinal. He found Bonaventure washing dishes. Receiving the news calmly, Bonaventure then told the messenger: "Hang the red hat on a tree until I have finished with the dishes!"

Other words on inspiration from Bonaventure:

- Spiritual joy and happiness is the surest sign of divine grace in the soul.
- The perfection of a religious man is to do perfect things in a common manner.
- True delight can only be found in God—it is this delight we seek.
- Since true happiness can only be found by the highest goodness and that is God...you cannot be truly happy unless you go beyond yourself, not with your body, but with your heart.
- In our prayers, what must be heard is not what comes out of our mouths, but what comes from our hearts.
- If you want to know about true beauty...ask for grace, not learning; desire, not comprehension... ask God, not man.

JULY 16
Mary Magdalen Postel
(d. 1846)

EARLY IN LIFE MARY MAGDALEN OPENED A SCHOOL for girls but soon the French Revolution stopped her work. During this period she made a secret chapel in her house where Mass was offered by priests who refused to swear allegiance to the secular government. In 1805, armed with her reputation but no money, she opened a school in Cherbourg; this was the origin of the Sisterhood of Christian Schools.

⁓

Many trials, setbacks, and crosses attended the growth of Mary Magdalen's order. Once when one of their group died, a rumor spread that she had died of starvation. Their sponsoring bishop then threw up his hands and told the community it was time to give up. Mary Magdalen thought differently, saying "I am so certain that Our Lord desires the realization of my aims that I shall not cease to pursue them with the greatest ardor. He who has given my daughters to me and who watches over the birds of the air can easily provide me with the means to support them."

JULY 18

Pambo

(d. 390)

A DISCIPLE OF SAINT ANTONY and a founder of the Nitrian group of monasteries in the deserts of Egypt.

A generous donor had given Pambo a valuable silver vessel which weighed some three hundred pounds. Never lifting his head to acknowledge the expensive gift, he told his steward to go and sell it so the proceeds could be given to the poor. The donor was speechless, expecting some notion of recognition or thanks, "Father do you know what I have just given you, how expensive a present it is?" Pambo's reply was uttered without a blink: "The one to whom it was offered does not need you to tell him its worth."

Pambo was given gold to distribute as alms among the poor. "Count it," said the donor. He replied: "God does not ask how much...not the amount, but the will when it is given."

A common saying from Pambo: "Keep your conscience free of offense to your neighbor and you will be saved." Also, "If you have a generous heart, you will have salvation."

Pambo's own religious exercises involved control over his tongue and the refraining from useless speech. Sharply reprimanded when he wouldn't speak to an allegedly corrupt bishop, he stated: "If he won't learn a lesson from my silence, my words won't teach him anything either!"

JULY 19
Arsenius the Great
(d. c.450)

ARSENIUS ABANDONED HIS POSITION AT COURT in Constantinople to join the monks in Alexandria, taking to the desert in disgust over people's weakness of character. He spent the rest of his life there.

~

Arsenius felt that formal education was unimportant, yet stated: "I know a great deal of Latin and Greek....I still have a great deal to learn in the alphabet of how to be a saint."

When he was, much to his dismay, visited by educated Romans, they were amazed at the degree of contemplation reached by the illiterate Egyptians. Arsenius replied: "We make no headway because we remain on the exterior which gives us pride...but the illiterate Egyptians have a true feeling for their weaknesses, blindness and insufficiencies."

Arsenius was known for his simple maxims. Included in the list of well-known sayings is the following, which he often repeated: "I always have something to repent for when I have spoken, but never when I have held my tongue!"

JULY 20
Gregory Lopez
(d. 1596)

A NATIVE OF MADRID, Gregory migrated to Mexico and lived there as a hermit among the Indians. Gregory's life as a solitary was marked by careful use of what was available rather than excessive "going without." He also wrote a book on the medicinal use of herbs for hospitals.

～

Gregory naturally spent long hours in prayer. Once, when asked about those who were able to enjoy a peaceful union with God through prayer, he said: "They are on a good path. But perfection does not lie in acts of enjoyment, but in the soul's effort to use all her forces in loving God in the most perfect way and with the most perfect acts of which one is capable."

JULY 22
Augustine Fangi
(d. 1493)

THE SON OF NOBLE PARENTS, Augustine was charmed by the Dominicans and joined their ranks. His reputation for penance was remarkable. He not only inflicted harsh punishments upon himself, he also patiently endured what life came to offer him.

This story is told about Augustine: Once, it is reported, he had to have surgery. He accepted this as a sign and another occasion to show penance, deciding to undergo the procedure without the benefit of anesthetic, which he did without a sound. It was said that his mind was so focused that he barely noticed what was being done to him!

JULY 23
John Cassian
(d. 433)

JOHN, AN ABBOT AND FOUNDER of two monasteries in Marseilles, was a follower of Saint John Chrysostom. From his monastic foundations, the spirit and ideal of Egyptian asceticism arose.

~

John is reported to have given the following counsel: "This is advice that is always in season....A monk should, at all costs, flee from the society of bishops and women; for neither women nor bishops permit a monk to remain at peace in his cell, nor fix his eyes on pure and heavenly doctrine."

JULY 24
Christina the Astonishing
(d. 1224)

BORN NEAR LIÈGE, Christina had an epileptic fit and thereafter experienced a lifelong series of paranormal experiences which were duly recorded by a contemporary.

~

The story is told that Christina "died" after a seizure at the age of twenty-two. During her Requiem Mass, just after the *Agnus Dei*, she sat up in her coffin and then flew to the rafters, "like a bird." Everyone in attendance, except her older sister and the priest, fled the church in fear. The priest convinced her to come down from the rafters—it is reported that she took refuge there because she was repelled by the smell of sinful humans. Speaking later of her death experience, she attested to the fact that she had truly died, having visited hell, seeing many of her friends. Returning to purgatory, she was offered the choice of remaining there or returning to earth. Liberated by the prayers of still more friends who were in purgatory, she decided to return.

JULY 31

John Colombini
(d. 1367)

A SUCCESSFUL MERCHANT, John's conversion was abrupt and astonishing. He changed his ways from a life as a conspicuous consumer, to that of a donor, even going to the extent of buying goods for more than their posted price and selling them for less than their value. Much to the chagrin of his wife, he tended to lepers, bringing them to his family's home, to his own bed. The first of these, it is written, miraculously disappeared from his home, leaving only a heavenly fragrance in his place.

John's wife, quite taken aback by the extreme degree of his conversion, asked him to temper his ministrations. He replied: "You prayed to God so that I might become a good, charitable man, now you are angry because I have so become and am making amends for my past sins!" Her quick retort was: "I prayed for rain and God sent me a flood!"

Ignatius of Loyola
(d. 1556)

FOUNDER OF THE SOCIETY OF JESUS (JESUITS), Ignatius was a Spanish soldier whose war wounds led to a retreat-convalescence that converted his mind to the service of the Church. Under Ignatius, the original band of ten companions spread throughout the world.

∼

Ignatius fancied himself an expert chef and gave the following instructions to the monastery cook: "You don't salt food in just any haphazard way—add half of the salt to the water to cook the meat when it begins to boil, one quarter during the cooking and the remaining quarter after it is cooked." He took great pleasure at seeing someone enjoy a meal with gusto, so he would go to great lengths to ensure that a hearty eater would be seated next to him during meals.

Saint Ignatius liked to pull pranks on his confreres. One of his companions was the type of person who liked to hear himself speak. After having heard that his friend had invited an older lady he met on the street to follow him if she "wanted to hear a good sermon," Ignatius knew just how to approach his friend when he needed a favor a few days later.

"Father, if you do this for me, I will personally bring another elderly lady to your next sermon!"

In discussions he had with Francis Xavier about founding a society that would be completely devoted to the salvation of souls, he often said: "What benefit will it be to a man if he gains the whole world but loses his soul in the process?"

Ignatius loved the game of pool and was so confident of his skill, he even made the following bet to a doctor of theology: "If you lose, I'll be your servant for thirty days; but if I win, you will do one thing that will be to your advantage." Thinking he had the better deal, the doctor agreed to the terms and the game begun. Of course, Ignatius won and, as the "loser," the doctor had to spend a month on retreat, reading Ignatius's *Spiritual Exercises*.

As general of the Jesuits, Ignatius also had to contend with menial matters. One such matter was the assignment of rooms for the priests. There just happened to be one priest who was never satisfied with his room, this time, it was too small. Ignatius finally decided to entertain his request, moving him to a larger room. Just one small aspect of this change had been overlooked, though, two other priests were also set to move into that same room with the priest who requested it!

Ignatius didn't hesitate using a little satire when correcting those who neglected or ill-performed their duties. Seeing a rather shoddy job had been done sweeping a corridor, Ignatius dressed a brother down: "Why are you sweeping this corridor?"

"For God and his love, your Reverence" was the smug, almost rote reply.

"Well, if you were doing it for man, that would be judged a bad job, but for God, it's insufferable!" was the saint's curt reply.

When Ignatius was imprisoned during the Inquisition for teaching "new ideas," he said: "I didn't know that it was a new idea to teach Christians about Christ!"

August

AUGUST 1
Alphonsus Liguori
(d. 1787)

Born in Naples, Alphonsus held a doctorate in both civil and ecclesiastical law. He was a lawyer, but left the bar in order to become a priest. Ordained at the age of thirty, he dedicated himself to an apostolate with the downtrodden and, in 1732, founded a Congregation (popularly known as the Redemptorists) devoted to the evangelization of the "most abandoned." In 1762, Pope Clement XIII forced him to accept the responsibilities of being a bishop. Saint Alphonsus pulled the Church away from fear and Jansenism: he opened it to hope but, above all, through his writings, he worked for the spread of Christian spirituality into all walks of life.

Thinking of himself to be a somewhat late bloomer, Alphonsus wanted to tell others not to waste time and get going early in life: He said: "When you see the value of the time you are losing, it will be too late to do anything about it!"

A composer in his own right, Alphonsus said: "If music isn't properly learned, not only is it not pleasurable, it is positively displeasing."

Remembering how his father Don Giuseppe had huge temper outbursts when he decided to quit law and enter the priesthood, Alphonsus wrote the following in a letter to his father after he had reduced another son, Ercole, to tears after a dispute: "For heaven's sake, end your dark moods...he is your son, not a dog!"

About parents' reactions to their offspring joining a religious order: "When leaving the world, one's worst enemies are his parents who, for either emotional or other personal reasons, they go against what God wants, and try to turn their children away from a vocation, a calling from God, rather than agree to it and give them permission."

AUGUST 2
Stephen I
(pope) (d. 257)

UPON HIS ELECTION TO THE HOLY SEE, Pope Stephen I had to face a controversy concerning the validity of baptism administered by heretics. He decided this question based on the tradition handed down by the early Church fathers. An unsubstantiated story says that the faction that did not agree with him managed to murder him while he sat on the papal chair during the celebration of the Eucharist.

~

Stephen's final edict was "let no innovation be introduced, but let us observe what is handed down to us by tradition." In that same vein, one of the maxims credited to him is this: "Antiquity keeps us as a possession, novelty is explosive."

John Vianney
(d. 1859)

JOHN VIANNEY WAS BORN IN DARDILLY, FRANCE, to a family who were good Catholics at a time when practicing the faith had to be done in a most secretive manner; priests risked their lives to bring the sacraments to the faithful because of the French Revolution and the restrictions placed on Catholics at that time.

John was ordained a priest in 1815, and in February 1818, the vicar general appointed him to a small parish of less than two hundred people in the village of Ars. Because of his no-nonsense, practical approach to his parishioners, he transformed a run-down village of sinful, non-practicing Catholics into a devoted, faith-filled group of believers. During his lifetime, people traveled from all corners of the world to confess their sins to him—to whom he offered simple, yet profound advice. To this day, Ars opens its doors to hundreds of thousands of pilgrims weekly.

~

A priest from a nearby parish asked Father Vianney: "Is it true that you give light penance to the greatest of sinners?"

Father Vianney answered: "We confessors also have to do our part."

One day, a visitor to Ars made the following comment: "Father, why can we barely hear you when you pray, but when you preach, you practically shout?"

Father replied: "When I preach, I often am speaking to those who are deaf to the word, or those who have fallen asleep, but when I pray, I am speaking to God—and I know that he's not deaf."

Father Vianney was often found to be in tears. A pilgrim asked him why. He answered: "I am crying over those things you should be crying about but don't."

Father Vianney was known for his austerities. Disgusted by the fuss made over meals, he dismissed his cook and asked a local widow to cook him a pot of potatoes once a week and leave it on the back of his stove. From these, he would feed himself for the week.

Madame Renard, the local widow who took care of Father Vianney's household, finally convinced the priest to accept a fresh loaf of bread once a week. One week her weekly visit to the rectory was delayed, hence the fresh bread. Upon arriving, she noticed a rather raggedy beggar waiting in the kitchen.

"What are you doing here?" she asked.

He replied: "Waiting for my bread, you're a day late!"

Visibly shaken by this, she went to get Father Vianney. "What does he mean?"

Father replied: "Well, it just seemed logical…I give him the fresh bread and he gives me the stale crusts…he has no teeth and I have good ones. I just dunk them a little in my coffee and they're fine."

Father Vianney was renowned for his skills in the confessional. One day, a woman of means, dressed in the highest of style came to see him, asking for absolution. Father Vianney was heard to have responded: "Save your soul which has been lost to all of this worldliness? It would be such a shame to lose a soul so dear to Our Lord that has been dressed so well to visit Him!"

One of Father Vianney's favorite sayings was: "A world without children is like the heavens without stars!"

Father Vianney had always wanted to live a life of prayer and solitude in spite of his very public life in Ars. On at least three occasions, he "escaped" Ars, only to return, either because of the pleas of the mayor or the crowds of people who followed him to whatever destination he had chosen for his "hideout." He had also even made arrangements with the local cloistered friars to keep a cell for him, "just in case" he was ever successful in his middle of the night escapes.

On one of these occasions, as he "made a run for it" under the cover of night, he stopped to pray at one of the large crucifixes that are placed along the roads in France. He recounts the following conversation he had with Our Lord.

"Where are you going, John Vianney?"

"I am leaving Ars in order to be able to look for you in the solitude of the friary, Lord. I beg you, let me leave Ars," replied Vianney.

"Don't look for me in solitude, John, but in the very souls which my mercy has led to you. One single soul is worth more than all of the prayers you could possibly pray in solitude. Return to them, go back to your Church. Many wounded souls await the Good Samaritan there."

Father Vianney then returned once again to Ars and thanked the Lord for enlightening him in the darkness of his night.

Because of his weak constitution and his poor eating habits, Father Vianney fell ill. Pilgrims prayed for him, as did his own orphans and students, each offering a sacrifice for his return to health. The unbelievable noise caused by the multitude in prayer under his bedroom window led him to remark: "Such a great noise for such a poor old priest…but it is good to hear them praying….I want to live a few years longer, for if I die today, I will appear before the Lord with empty hands!"

All his life, John Vianney was able to laugh heartily at his own lack of talent. Even when he was a student for the priesthood, John didn't take himself too seriously. A professor who examined John before his ordination was exasperated with his seeming dullness said: "This fellow is a complete ass. What can he possibly accomplish?"

Vianney overheard the professor and replied, "If Samson, armed only with the jawbone of an ass, could kill one thousand Philistines, imagine what God could do with a complete ass!"

A person seeking his advice, asked Vianney, "How should I go to God?" Vianney answered: "Go straight!"

A very chubby wealthy lady asked Vianney what was needed so she could get into heaven. He replied: "About three Lenten fasts!"

AUGUST 6
Schetzelon
(d. 1141)

A HERMIT who lived in the woods near Luxembourg, Schetzelon subsisted on acorns and roots. The farmers came to know him and left pieces of stale bread for the hermit, knowing that he would have refused anything that was fresh. Out of respect for the life he had chosen, they never tried to speak to him, nor to see him. His stated aim in life was to live without superfluities. When asked if he had experienced many temptations during his life, he replied: "Yes, the life of man is one long series of temptations." When he died, a chapel was built in his honor which drew pilgrims. The water at his spring was blessed each year.

~

Schetzelon's clothing was so sparse it is said that Saint Bernard sent him a shirt and a pair of pants made by his monks. Out of respect, Schetzelo put them on, but immediately removed them, saying that they were luxuries he didn't need.

Avoiding distractions in prayer is not always easy, even for a hermit. One day snow fell overnight covering Schetzelon entirely—except for his face. A freezing hare found that warm spot and settled comfortably on the hermit's face. The hermit's first reaction was laughter. Quickly, the hermit realized his mistake—when he should have been praying, he was playing with a rabbit under the snow.

AUGUST 7
Cajetan
(d. 1547)

CAJETAN, THE CO-FOUNDER of the Theatine Clerks Regular, toiled endlessly for the recognition of his Order. Unrest ruled, Rome was attacked, and the Theatine house was destroyed. Consequently, the Theatines made their way to Venice where the situation was also desperate. Cajetan was also called to attend to matters in Naples, where he died, worn out by his efforts at reformation.

~

A large estate was offered to Cajetan by a rich merchant from Venice who wished to establish the Theatines there. With Cajetan's refusal came this reply: "It is true that you may be richer than merchants in Naples, but God is the same in both places."

Cajetan's primary focus was the spiritual life of his Oratorians, but his equally as important apostolate was tending to the incurably ill: "In the oratory, we try to serve God through worship, but in the hospital, we actually find him."

Cajetan was becoming weaker, his health was failing. He had to handle so many things—civil disobedience and calamity in Naples, the Protestants, and his disappointment at the Council of Trent. He took to his bed, his last breath within sight. When his doctors advised him not to lie on the hard boards of the cot, but to use a mattress, his reply was sharp: "My Savior died on a cross, at least allow me to die on a plank of wood!"

AUGUST 8
Altman
(d. 1091)

BISHOP OF PASSAU, Altman upheld the laws governing celibacy of priests. He was chased from his diocese, a revolt that was led by his own clergy. Though driven from his see, Altman continued to exercise great influence. He was buried at the Benedictine abbey in Austria which he founded.

~

Returning to his see repeatedly towards the end of his life, Altman sold all that he owned to repair the primarily wooden churches there. His biographer tells us of his comments at that time: "Many of my churches are made of wood, so are many of my priests....I find that it is more difficult to reform the clergy than their buildings."

Edith Stein

(d. 1942)

BORN IN POLAND, the youngest in a large Jewish family, a brilliant student (earning a Ph.D. by the age of twenty-five), she converted to Catholicism in 1922. Eleven years later, she entered the Carmelites and took the name Saint Teresa Benedicta of the Cross. An insightful spiritual writer, Edith was sent to Holland for safety's sake and, along with her sister, Rose, was arrested when the Nazis invaded and conquered that country. She was sent to a concentration camp at Auschwitz and died in its gas chambers in 1942. She was canonized in 1998.

～

In 1904, Edith, who was a Jew at the time, confessed her strong desire to her mother to convert to Catholicism and become a Carmelite sister. Her mother rushed to take her to services in a neighboring synagogue. After services, she questioned Edith: "Wasn't that sermon beautiful? Didn't the Rabbi touch your heart?"

Edith replied: "Yes, of course."

Her mother asked: "Then you agree, you can still be religious and be a Jew?"

The reply came: "Undoubtedly...if I knew nothing else!"

Here is Sister Teresa Benedicta's advice on living a day at a time: "Take everything you have within yourself and put it completely into God's hands at the end of each day. Don't be embarrassed or ashamed, just take everything as is...leave it with him and then you will be able to rest in him and start the next day as a new life."

Laurence

(d. 258)

A DEACON OF THE ROMAN CHURCH, Laurence was responsible for caring for the Church's goods and distributing alms to the poor. Laurence was probably beheaded by Roman persecutors, but a life of this popular figure was written a century later and inspired his wide veneration in both East and West.

~

Laurence was called to court by the Roman prefect who had been informed of the "riches" of the Christians and who demanded that Laurence produce them. Thinking this amounted to a considerable treasure, the prefect wanted these riches for his own coffers. The prefect furthered his argument, saying that he knew the Christian doctrine stated that "they must render to Caesar what is his." Laurence replied that the Church was indeed very rich and that no treasure could even come close to its value. Offering to show him just a small part, he asked for an adequate amount of time so he could make an inventory. Naturally, the prefect did not understand what types of riches Laurence meant. "You have three days" was the prefect's answer.

During this time, Laurence went throughout the city, seeking the ill, handicapped, orphans, widows and maidens—the treasure of the Church. He assembled these people on the third day before the prefect who was surprised to see such a downtrodden assembly of people. "Where are these treasures of which you speak? All I see is a group of people, needy people at that!" the prefect said. Laurence replied: "These are the treasures of the Church!" The prefect replied: "You are mocking me...you shall die...inch by inch!"

An enormous gridiron was built and hot coals were laid underneath in readiness for Laurence's torturous death sentence. He was bound to it. After having suffered for a long time, Laurence turned to one of his executioners and said: "Turn me, that side is done enough." Shortly afterwards, Laurence said: "I am cooked enough," he then closed his eyes and went home to the Lord.

AUGUST 12

Innocent XI
(pope) (d. 1689)

BENEDETTO ODESCALCHI WAS ESPECIALLY KNOWN for his simple deep piety, charity, and devotion both before and after his election to the Holy See. A staunch opponent of King Louis XIV's involvement in church affairs, Innocent's entire term as pope was marked by a continuous battle to reduce the king's influence. As pope, he wanted religious instruction to be given to all and passed strict laws against nepotism in the clergy and against gambling.

~

With respect to his brother-priests, he was quite harsh, stating: "We therefore likewise establish that no one be able to be chosen a prelate or superior if he frequently rides horseback...who uses undergarments or shirts or linens upon himself or on his bed, or one who goes about with shoes... who has been seen at anytime handling money...or who notably is defective in attending the community choir, refectory, and other places, as is prescribed...."

John Berchmanns

(d. 1621)

ONE OF FIVE CHILDREN BORN TO A SHOEMAKER, three of whom entered the religious life, he spent a great deal of time caring for his ailing mother. He decided he wanted to become a Jesuit after reading about the life of Saint Aloysius Gonzaga. He studied the main languages spoken in Europe, since his dream was to help and teach immigrants. He died, of unknown causes, clutching his rosary, crucifix and book of rules, after participating in a public debate defending the faith. He did not live to be ordained.

~

Fittingly, John announced that "if I do not become a saint when I am young, I will never become one."

On holiness, John has said: "The path to holiness lies in the ordinary, rather than the extraordinary."

John was rather taken back by his physician's prescription to cure his illness: bathe the forehead using vintage wine. His curt response was: "It's fortunate that I am dying, I can't afford such an expensive disease."

Benildus

(d. 1862)

BENILDUS, PETER ROMANÇON PRIOR TO ENTERING the religious Order of the Brothers of Christian Schools, was a well-loved teacher who ran the local school for girls. Members of the local parish church said of him: "Brother Benildus did not worship God like an angel only when he was praying in church, but everywhere and all of the time...even among his cabbages in the garden!"

~

Brother Benildus often said that he loved all of the congregation, even when they forced him to "eat potato skins" (which happened when they hadn't paid him for his teaching).

It took Benildus at least three tries to be accepted as a novice. His rejection was due to his small stature. He took this in stride, stating: "God calls to me and he knows how tall I am...and it is not important to him....He created me this size....When will these men realize that size is of no importance?"

AUGUST 17
Joan Delanoue
(d. 1736)

YOUNGEST OF TWELVE CHILDREN and daughter of a merchant of religious artifacts at a shrine at Ardilliers, France, Joan became the sole heir to the family business when her parents died. She founded the Sisters of Saint Anne after a long career as a shopkeeper. Originally almost stingy, Joan would send her niece shopping for food while she herself was eating, so that she could truthfully tell beggars there was no food in the house.

~

Joan's conversion came as the result of an uncharacteristic act of charity—she took in an old beggar lady who showed Joan the way to true happiness, telling her that her job was giving, not taking. At one point, Joan received a vision of her future in which she was told that there were six children, abandoned and cold, who needed her help. This vision was true, she took the children in and, within three years, she had set up an orphanage, calling it Providence House. The local citizens wondered where the money came from that supported the orphanage. Only Joan knew the answer: "The King of France won't give us any money from his purse, but the King of all kings will always keep his purse open for us."

AUGUST 19
John Eudes
(d. 1680)

ORDAINED AS A MEMBER OF THE ORATORIANS, John risked his life to aid the victims of the plague in France. In 1641, he founded the Congregation of Our Lady of Charity to prevent women and girls from taking up a life of prostitution. Later, he established the Society of Jesus and Mary (the Eudists), dedicated to the education of priests and missionary work, and the Society of the Heart of the Mother Most Admirable (resembling the third orders of Saint Francis). He was also the author of many books. During his lifetime, Father Eudes preached missions in various parts of France.

John took two missionaries to task for refusing to hear the confession of a beggar. He said to them: "I wonder if you'd mind hearing the confessions of two lovely young ladies, who are still waiting at the door for you?"

The missionaries replied, as they looked out the window for the two young ladies: "Gladly, where are they?"

John said: "That's all I wanted to know."

One of the most "preeminent" preachers, John saw his job as one of going from the pulpit to the confessional: "For the preacher beats the bushes, but the confessors catch the birds."

AUGUST 20
Bernard of Clairvaux
(d. 1153)

BORN THE THIRD OF SEVEN SONS to a family in Burgundy, Bernard was educated with particular care because a devout man had, before his birth, foretold his great destiny. A Doctor of the Church, during his lifetime he founded one hundred sixty-three monasteries in different parts of Europe. He was an advisor to popes and kings, the first Cistercian monk to be placed on the calendar of saints.

~

Bernard of Clairvaux and his fellow Cistercians, while opening a new abbey in Foigny, were attacked by a horde of flies. They were unable to swat them all away. Finally, Bernard solemnly told the flies: "I hereby excommunicate you!" The next day, every single fly was found dead on the floor.

A priest came to see Bernard to express his anger because he wasn't admitted to Bernard's order. "What good is recommending perfection in your books, if you won't let people who are perfect seek it in your order? If I had one of your books here now, I would rip it to shreds!"

Bernard replied: "I think you haven't read my books very carefully, for I remember that I recommended that for one to become perfect, he must make a change in his morals, not his location."

It is said that Bernard was so charismatic a figure that the women hid their sons, boyfriends, and husbands when they heard he was coming for fear that he would turn them into monks.

Pius X

(pope) (d. 1914)

GIUSEPPE SARTO WAS ONE OF EIGHT CHILDREN born to a poor shoemaker and his wife. An exceptional student, his calling became evident to him at a young age. Ordained in 1858, he worked tirelessly to establish night schools for adults, restoring churches, and ministering to the poor and sick. After several religious postings, Cardinal Sarto was elected pope in 1903.

~

As Pope Pius X, he issued decrees on early communion (at age seven instead of age fourteen). He reformed the liturgy, promoting clear and simple homilies, bringing the Gregorian chant back to services. He revised the Breviary and instituted teaching of the catechism. He reorganized the Roman Curia, working against modernism. He initiated the codification of canon law and promoted Bible reading by all. It is reported that his final will and testament read: "I was born poor; I lived poor; I wish to die poor."

One day, as the Pope was entering the basilica in the Vatican, great applause broke out spontaneously. Pius X seemed rather disturbed and commented to a fellow prelate saying, in a loud voice: "We do not applaud the servant in the Master's house."

After having seen a dozen oil paintings of himself, believing each to be worse than the previous one, Pope Pius X returned to his room, leaving his aides to cool their heels in the papal library.

After a period of time, Pius returned and explained to his aides: "I went to my room to take a look at myself in a mirror to see if I am really as ugly as they have painted me to be. Judging this to be true, I leave the choice of my official portrait up to you."

Unlike others, Pius did not come out against the use of snuff, which is powdered tobacco. When his physicians had brought to his attention that the previous pope, Leo XIII, had given it up in the later years of his life, he retorted: "Come back and see me again when I'm ninety-three...that's when I'll give it up!"

Pius seemed to be a groundbreaker in a number of areas. One evening, Pius asked one of his secretaries to dine with him. When he was told that it was customary for the Pope to dine alone, he asked: "Who made this into a custom?"

The answer came back: "Urban VIII set the rule."

"Well, if Urban can make a rule that became a custom, certainly Pius X can abolish it!"

A story comes to us about what happened during the religion class of the future Pius X. The teacher-priest challenged: "I'll give two apples to any student who can tell me where God is."

Giuseppi Sarto (the future pope) replied: "I'll give two apples to anyone who can tell me where he isn't."

Pius X used to play word games with his name which was Giuseppi Sarto. In Italian, the word *sarto* means "tailor." Once, a pretentious man was vying for the pontiff's friendship with the hopes of an episcopal appointment. Pius X pushed him away, saying: "I will not give him a hat….I'm a tailor, not a milliner." On yet another occasion, a woman approached him saying that she had heard he was a saint. Pius smiled and said: "My dear woman, my name is Sarto, not Santo."

Common opinion was that Pius X was a saint. To this, he replied: "Don't I already have enough to do? Now they want miracles, too!"

Pius X did not like the practice of kissing the Pope's foot and decided he would abolish it. When one of the cardinals tried to kiss his foot, he said: "My friend, don't do that— I'm scared I'll kick you in the nose!" Needless to say, the practice was never resumed.

AUGUST 23
Rose of Lima
(d. 1617)

THE PATRONESS OF THE AMERICAS, the first saint born there (Lima, Peru, to Spanish immigrants), her real name was Isabel, but it was changed to Rose because she was such a beautiful baby. Aware of this beauty and the problems it could cause, she is reported to have rubbed lye and pepper on her face in order to cause its disfigurement.

Devoting herself completely to Jesus, she was a mystic and received invisible stigmata. She built a cell in which to live in her garden, where she raised vegetables and did embroidery as well as other needlework to support her poor parents. Her nights were spent in prayer and penance, and she practiced severe self-mortifications. She received the habit of Saint Dominic at the age of twenty.

~

There was a religious brother who was a smoker: not just a regular smoker, but someone who had a passion for smoking. He would practice his passion, his love for tobacco, in such a way that it was not only injurious to everyone around him (as well as himself), he was a nuisance. It is reported that his mouth and nose were black like a chimney, a dark cloud surrounded his brain and his lungs emitted such hoarse asthmatic rasps, it was often thought that the man would die during one of his numerous choking fits. But he still smoked, never removing his pipe from between his lips. His doctor advised him to quit, so did his friends and his religious superiors—they issued numerous censures and punishments to no avail, all was in vain. No threat or penalty could end his habit.

One day, he went to see Rose, who was an excellent milliner, because he needed to have a special collar made. In the midst of his smoke, he blurted and coughed out his story. She stated that she would pray on it. After five days of Rose's prayers, the religious brother was smoke-free and remained as such for the remainder of his life!

Rose's parents had a young cockerel they had hoped to breed for a fee. Everyone in the household loved the bird and constantly gave it treats. It grew fat and lazy, strutting around, stopping only to bask in the sunshine, but refusing to crow. Tiring of this behavior and fearing no return for their investment, Rose's mother brought the bird into the kitchen and set it onto the table saying: "Either you crow, or we'll slit your throat and eat you tomorrow!" Rose, touched by this, said to the bird: "Crow, my dear cockerel, and you'll not die." Scarcely had these words come from her lips when the bird stood up, shook his wings, stiffened his neck so that his comb became a bright scarlet and crowed loudly. Everyone burst out laughing—the more they laughed, the louder he crowed. With stately strides, he strutted to Rose, thrust his head to her, uttering the most vociferous sounds anyone had heard—and he didn't stop for a full week!

AUGUST 25

Louis IX, King of France
(d. 1270)

LOUIS IX WAS GRANTED all the characteristics that made a king great—good looks, wealth, heroism, and piety. The son of Louis VIII and Blanche, his mother took his education in hand— often uttering to Louis: "I love you so much my son, as much as a mother could...but I'd rather see you dead than have you commit a mortal sin." Crowned at the age of twelve, with his mother as regent, he became known for his sense of justice and great love for the Church. When he came of age in 1235, Louis took control of his kingdom.

~

On the subject of marriage, Louis believed that only generosity through self-sacrifice could keep love alive over time. He said: "In the absence of self-sacrifice, married life is reduced to two months of *honey*moon and fifty years of *bitter*moon."

On the subject of his mode of dress, Louis's wife was very critical. She felt that he dressed in a style that was much too austere, far below his station in life. In response to her incessant comments, one day, he replied: "I am as displeased with your own flamboyant taste in clothes and jewelry as you are with my austerities. As soon as you tone down your ways, I'll improve my own."

Louis was an informal person. As saintly and royal as he was, he enjoyed the art of spirited conversation with whoever were his companions of the moment. One evening, after supper at a local monastery, when the monks offered to read to him from some learned passages, as was their custom, Louis's reply was clear: "You can find no book that interests me as much as a good spontaneous lively conversation where everyone says exactly what he thinks, no matter what."

AUGUST 26

Bernard of Offida

(d. 1694)

SENT TO HERD SHEEP AT THE AGE OF SEVEN, Bernard heard the call of God and joined the Capuchins as a lay brother in 1626. He practiced his faith with great zeal, often distributing more alms to the poor than the community could afford. Later, he was given the job as a gatherer of alms—the abbot felt that he could teach him an important lesson—but to no avail. Bernard died at the age of ninety.

~

Bernard's reputation as a giver of good advice, consolation, and help created another problem in the community, for people would often call upon him, asking for a miracle. One day, a woman, carrying her very ill baby, came to see him, seeking a cure. Bernard took the child in his arms, all the while trying to explain that he was not in charge of miracles, that they came from the Lord. The woman grabbed onto his habit and wouldn't let go. The child died in his arms. Bernard, the child in his arms, with the woman hanging onto his habit, dragged the duo to the church. He laid the baby on the altar dedicated to Saint Felix and exclaimed: "Now my good saint, this is the time to help me." Finishing his plea with a prayer, he looked up and the child was alive and well (and the woman had let go of his habit).

Poemen
(d. *c*.450)

POEMEN WAS AN EGYPTIAN, aged fifteen, when he became an anchorite in Scete. He was a master of fasting—first every day, then, later in life, eating one small meal a day. His advice on fasting was: "Never eat to your hunger, always leave the table hungry—this is the royal road that leads to salvation"; "we do not fast to kill our bodies, but to kill our passions"; "a monk should never fast for a long period of time for then he proudly views it as an achievement—eating a small dinner daily prevents the sin of pride, but it also makes him feel his hunger, right to the very core of his gut."

~

A hermit once told Poemen: "When a brother, who is a pious man, comes to see me, I receive him with joy; but if another brother, who has fallen away from belief, comes, I shut the door in his face."

Poemen replied: "You have done wrong—for those who are sick in the soul need the gentle hands of the nurse and the tender care of the hospital; throw open your door and spread your arms to the sinner."

When anyone complained to Poemen that the devil tormented him and he felt lost, Poemen would reply: "You always know exactly where the devil is...below you!"

A monk asked Poemen: "I have a neighbor to whom I do good deeds—but I constantly feel that these deeds are sprinkled with self-satisfaction, or some other self-serving motive is mixed up with my intent. Do I continue to do these deeds?"

Poemen replied in the form of a small story: "There were two men who had two fields. One sowed a crop of corn in which was mixed tares (corn weeds), the other did nothing. When it came to harvesttime, the former had a mixed crop— some of it was good, some bad—but he took the time to sort the corn from the weeds. The latter had nothing but useless weeds. Who acted best?"

Poemen made the following comment about temptations: "Flee from all, but if you must face them, show the bold double-edge of the sword of the Spirit....Some temptations must be taken by the throat, like David killed the lion.... Others must be strangled, like David hugged the bear to death....Some are best kept to yourself, but don't give them any air, shut them in a bottle like scorpions, for their stings are just as dangerous."

AUGUST 27

Monica

(d. 387)

MOTHER OF SAINT AUGUSTINE OF HIPPO, Monica was given in marriage to a bad-tempered pagan. She prayed constantly for his conversion and that of her fun-loving son. The former was converted on his deathbed, the latter after sowing some wild oats of his own, producing an illegitimate son. A reformed alcoholic, she was a pious woman who prayed constantly.

~

One day, when no one was around, a housemaid had a rather harsh argument with the diminutive Monica. Taking this in as a sign, she commented: "I have seen my own error, I have condemned it and have given it up. In the same way that a friend's flattery can pervert someone, the insult of an enemy can be used as a means of correction....But you, Lord, chose this young maid as an instrument to reprimand me for my wrongdoing so that I could make amends to you."

With incredible intuition, Monica commented to her son, Augustine: "A little knowledge turns one away from God....A great deal of knowledge brings one back to him."

When explaining that a truly happy man is not just one who has everything he desires, Monica stated: "If he desires what is good and has it, that's fine, then he is happy. But if what he wants is evil and gets it, he is unhappy. A person is less unhappy not getting what he wants than if he desires something that is evil."

Monica said: "God is everywhere, even with sinners. It is not enough to have God in us to be happy, he must also be our friend."

AUGUST 28
Augustine of Hippo
(d. 430)

BORN IN AFRICA, *the son of the Christian Monica and the pagan Patricius, he experienced an almost miraculous conversion while in Milan. Later the bishop of Hippo, Augustine is a Doctor of the Church, having written numerous volumes, among which are his* Confessions *and the* City of God.

~

Continuing his mother Monica's comments about true happiness, Augustine said: "Anyone who loves and possesses a perishable good could never be truly happy, for they fear the loss of it...even if they were sure that it would never be lost...for one earthly desire leads to another, and to another, and so on."

Speaking of chastity, Augustine said: "A soul is truly chaste only if it keeps its gaze fixed upon God, grasping onto only him."

About sensual pleasure: "The only pleasure one gets from doing something that is evil is in knowing that it is evil...that pleasure is fleeting, for it soon grows tiresome and common-place."

Augustine has written these sage comments:

- "The ideal of man is to live in peace and die in serenity."
- "The devil invented gambling."
- "When people ask God for a long life, what are they asking for but increasing infirmity?"
- "When a person loves worldly goods, it is a kind of bird leavings that wrap the soul up and stop it from taking flight to God.
- "No one is truly happy if he has what he wants, but only if he wants something he should have."

Aidan

(d. 651)

Very little is known of his life with the exception that he was a monk from Ireland. All who found themselves traveling with him, on foot, of course, had to either read the Bible or learn the psalms by heart. He had little care for worldly goods and was known for his great charity. Appointed bishop, he was a great proponent of the welfare of children and slaves. It is said that he died standing up, leaning against the wall of his church mission center while they were raising a tent for him.

⁓

The lengthy fast of Lent over, Aidan was exuberant to be sharing the Easter feast with Oswald, the king. The king himself, expressing his own gladness, added an extra "amen" when he smelled the long-missed fragrance of cooked meat. A number of others were also attending this feast, although in the courtyard—the poor, homeless, and starving. Knowledge of these "guests" soon reached the king's ears at which point, without hesitation, he ordered his servants to "take the meat outside and distribute it among our guests there… and take this silver dish as well…break it into little pieces and divide it among the poor people." Aidan was so happy to see such an act of charity from the king that he grabbed the king's right hand and cried: "May this royal hand never see corruption!" History proves that his petition really came true in every respect—Oswald's reign was never touched by any form of corruption.

One day, as a gesture of love, King Oswine, successor to King Oswald, gave him a royal horse so that if the need arose, Aidan could travel quickly to tend to urgent business.

Being the generous soul that he was, Aidan gave the magnificent animal to the first beggar he saw who needed transportation. News of this came to Oswine as he was entering his dining room for lunch; he was hurt, puzzled, and then burst into a red-hot rage as he met Aidan at the entrance. "My Lord Bishop, whatever possessed you to give away such a magnificent royal horse to a beggar? You know that it was a gift I specially selected and gave you for your own needs....Are there no cheaper horses which could have done the job for him?" The bishop stopped and thought for a moment before he spoke, then said: "Your Highness, what is your answer, is a mare's colt of more value than a child of God?" The King thought for time, followed the Bishop into the dining room, and then knelt at his feet, asking his forgiveness: "Forgive me for my anger and rudeness. I will never again say anything about it, no matter how much of our money you give to these children of God."

September

~

SEPTEMBER 1
Lupus of Sens (d. 623)

A MONK WHO BECAME BISHOP OF SENS, Lupus was forced out of his diocese by slander. He was later vindicated.

~

Lupus said: "The ugly words of men count for nothing when your conscience is clear."

SEPTEMBER 3
Gregory the Great
(pope) (d. 604)

THE SON OF A WEALTHY ROMAN SENATOR and Saint Silvia, he was trained to be a lawyer by the finest professors available in Rome at the time. Appointed prefect of Rome, after a year he sold all of his possessions, turned the family mansion into a Benedictine monastery, quit his official duties, and became a Benedictine monk. When he was elected pope unanimously in 590, he set his sights on evangelization, sending missionaries to England, France, Spain, and Africa. He was the creator of what we now know as Gregorian chant. He is considered one of the great Doctors of the Latin Church.

~

Pope Gregory was walking around Rome when he spotted some handsome, light-skinned young men for sale at the market place. Making an inquiry, he found out that the men were from Britain and had never heard about Christianity before. He commented: "It's a pity that such handsome men are servants of the prince of darkness. What are they called?... Angles?...That is rather appropriate, their faces are so like angels, one day, they will be united with the angels." The story continues that, in order to make these Angles into angels, he sent Saint Augustine and forty other monks to their native Britain.

Gregory's comments on love are appropriate today: "The proof we have that love exists is by loving. Where there is love, great things happen. But when love stops acting, it ceases to exist."

Here is Gregory's take on saving repentance for last: "If we knew ahead of time when we were going to depart from this world, we could choose a season for pleasure and another to repent. But God, who has promised to pardon all of our sins if we are truly repentant, has never promised a tomorrow. So, we must always think that this day is our last, our last chance to repent and change our ways. But we still hold the notion that we have time left to us. Not only do we not weep for the sins we have committed, we add to the list."

Gregory reminds us that even our good deeds come from God: "If we do good deeds, we must remember that our strength to do them comes from God. We can't rely on our own strength, since we may not have a tomorrow. No one should rejoice in having done good deeds...for as long as we experience the uncertainty of an earthly life, we do not know what will follow....We should never put any trust in our own virtue."

Gregory has this to say about the Scriptures: "The Holy Bible is like a mirror....In it, we see our interior face. From its Scriptures, we can spot our spiritual deformities as well as our beauty....There, we also discover the progress we are making towards perfection."

Cuthbert of Lindisfarne
(d. 687)

AS A YOUNG ORPHAN, Cuthbert became a shepherd and then a monk at Melrose Abbey, where he later was appointed prior. He engaged in missionary work and attracted huge crowds until he retired to live as a hermit. He became bishop of Lindisfarne and spent the last two years of his life caring for those who became ill of the plague that swept his diocese.

Always active in the service of his people, Cuthbert had been known to say: "What am I lying here for? God will certainly have heard the prayers of so many good men. Fetch me my coat and staff!"

About being disturbed during sleep he said, "One cannot displease me by waking me out of my sleep but, on the contrary, it gives me pleasure; for by rousing me from inactivity it enables me to do or think of something useful."

Lamenting his own temptations, Cuthbert said: "If I could live in a tiny dwelling on a rock in the ocean, surrounded by the waves of the sea and cut off from the sight and sound of everything else, I would still not be free of the cares of this passing world, or from the fear that somehow the love of money might still come and snatch me away."

SEPTEMBER 5
Laurence Justiniani
(d. 1456)

BORN INTO A PROMINENT VENETIAN FAMILY, Laurence was raised by his widowed mother. At the age of nineteen, Laurence had a vision of Eternal Wisdom. Relating this story to his uncle, an Augustinian canon, he suggested that Laurence assume the sacrifices of a monk at home prior to giving all his worldly goods up and entering the religious life. He took this advice and later, in 1406, was ordained a priest. Still later he was made superior of his congregation, then he was appointed bishop of Castello and, finally, served as archbishop of Venice. Laurence worked at restoring the faith of the people under his jurisdiction.

~

Laurence was unrelenting in his charity to the poor, even shorting his own personal budgets for his home, clothing, and food to see that all could be fed and clothed. It is interesting to mention that he never gave too much money to anyone at once, "Lest it be ill-managed." When a relative asked for help in providing a dowry for his daughter, Laurence replied: "A little wouldn't be enough for you. And if I gave you more, I would be robbing my poor."

On his deathbed, when offered a featherbed, he replied: "My Savior died on a wooden cross, a wooden bed is fine for my own death."

Laurence practiced severe austerities, eating only when necessary and never drinking outside of mealtime. When asked about his approach, Laurence commented: "If we cannot bear this small thirst, how will we endure purgatory, where we may be eternally parched?"

SEPTEMBER 7
Sozon
(d. 304)

Sozon was a Christian shepherd boy who, at a pagan celebration, pulled off the golden hand of an idol, broke it into pieces, and gave it to the poor. He was burned at the stake.

~

When brought before the Roman governor Maximian, he was asked to renounce Jesus and to worship pagan idols. Sozon refused so Maximian ordered that nails be driven into his shoes, and Sozon was made to walk into the arena in this condition. As he walked, blood spurted from his feet, coloring his skin up to his knees. As he continued to walk, Sozon spoke to Maximian, saying: "You are not as gaily booted as I am—in royal crimson!"

SEPTEMBER 9
Peter Claver
(d. 1654)

The son of a farmer, he studied at the University of Barcelona. A Jesuit priest by the age of twenty, he ministered to the physical and spiritual needs of the slaves in the Americas. It is reported that he converted more than three hundred thousand souls while working with them on the plantations for some forty years (mainly in Cartegna). He is compared to Saint Vincent de Paul since he organized similar charitable organizations, but the difference was that Peter's were founded for the blacks in the Americas.

~

Peter was always being bothered because the places where he did his holy work were not necessarily the most ideal. Concerns were met with the remark: "I have no sense of taste, but I do have a strong stomach....If that makes a person a saint, well I guess I am one!"

On one occasion when Peter was complimented on his apostolic zeal, his reply was: "It is as it should be, but I'm afraid there is some self-indulgence in this, for it comes from my natural enthusiasm....If it were not for this work, I would be a nuisance to myself and everyone else!"

SEPTEMBER 11
Paphnutius
(d. 350)

AN ACTIVE PARTICIPANT in the Council of Nicea in 525, he suffered mutilation of his left leg and the loss of his right eye while being tortured for the faith. Paphnutius was subsequently condemned to the mines. It is said that this Egyptian anchorite lived to well over the age of ninety. He was eventually martyred by the Prefect Culcianus.

~

Paphnutius, when giving his opinion about married clergy, commented: "Do not lay this heavy yoke on the clergy. Marriage is honorable, but the wives will suffer the most!"

John Chrysostom
(d. 407)

KNOWN AS THE GREATEST OF THE GREEK FATHERS, *he was raised by his very pious mother. Well educated, he studied under the most renowned thinkers of his era and became a monk, priest, then a preacher. He earned his title "Chrysostom," which means golden-mouthed, because of the eloquence of his sermons that were always precise and clear. Reluctantly accepting an appointment as the bishop of Constantinople, John was criticized because he would not partake of the riches of the office. He worked diligently for the reform of the clergy, preventing the sale of clerical offices, calling for fidelity in marriage and encouraging justice in all religious practices. He revised the Greek liturgy and is a Greek Father as well as a Doctor of the Church, proclaimed as such in 451. He is well known for his numerous writings: letters, homilies, and works of theology.*

John's advice on where to turn for help if God is punishing you is this: "When you realize that God is punishing you, don't flee to the enemy, go quickly to God's allies—the saints and martyrs, they will help you because they have great influence with him."

About starting an effective set of reforms, John said: One must "sweep the stairs beginning from the top" of the hierarchy.

On prayer: "One cannot possibly lead a virtuous life without prayer."

On the value of suffering: "If the Lord should give you the power to restore life, it would be a lesser gift than if he allows you to suffer. Through a miracle, you would be indebted to him, but through suffering, he is indebted to you."

On the cross: "Even men of no learning understood that the cross was persuasive, it persuaded the whole world."

On injuring the innocent: "If God punishes those who rejoice in the sufferings of their enemies, how much more will he punish those people who, excited by envy, look to injure those who have never done anything to them?"

SEPTEMBER 14
Notburga
(d. 1313)

NOTBURGA WAS AN INDENTURED SERVANT assigned to work in the fields. Little else is known of her history.

⁓

This is the most famous of the events of Notburga's legend: She was working in the fields and the bell rang for vespers, indicating the beginning of Sunday. Notburga began to leave in order to prepare for services. Her employer told her to keep on working, but she refused, saying that good Christians do not work on Sundays. She then laid down her sickle, saying to the farmer that there was no moon for light to work by. He replied: "Give me that sickle, I'll show you the moon," and proceeded to throw the tool to heaven where a crescent moon (the shape of the sickle) appeared. This story is sometimes told to explain origin of the crescent moon.

John the Dwarf

(fifth century)

A NATIVE OF LOWER EGYPT, John was a disciple of Poeman.
Very little is known of his early life, except that his small stat-
ure gave him the occasion to exercise a rather peppery temper.

∼

Early in his religious life, he told his elder brother, who
lived in the same cell as he did: "I want to be an angel so I
can live an angelic life in the desert." John retired to the
rocky wasteland near their community, but soon tired of the
austerity of this experiment. When he arrived back at his
brother's cell, it was evening. He knocked on the door but
was not admitted without identifying himself. He answered:
"It is I, your brother, John." His brother replied: "That could
not be, for my brother is no longer a man, he is now an
angel." John was forced to sleep outside that entire night. In
the morning, his brother went out and saw John crouching
at the doorstep: "How can this be? Why didn't you come
in? Angels can certainly pass through closed doors."

John gradually attained a measure of humility and got
his temper under control, becoming a model of obedience.
Soon, he had disciples who wished to learn obedience, for if
he could do it, so could they. One day, the boldest asked
what he could do to learn obedience. John answered "Do?
Go and take my cane, plant it and water it daily." The young
man did so, in spite of the fact that he had to fetch water
daily from a great distance. After a period of two years, the
stick sprouted roots, putting forth leaves, flowers, and then
a bountiful crop of scarlet berries, which he brought back to

show his master in church. John gathered a handful of these berries and said: "See, these are the fruits of holy obedience."

SEPTEMBER 16
Edith of Wilton
(d. 984)

THE ILLEGITIMATE DAUGHTER of King Edgar the Peaceable, she was raised in Wilton Abbey, which she never left. A Benedictine nun at the age of fifteen, she built the Saint Denis Church in Wilton.

⁓

When discussing a possible change in the style of habits for her burgeoning religious community, a change to which she was opposed, Edith said to her bishop: "One's mind may be as modest under street garments as it is under a habit. My God looks not at how I dress, but into my heart. God can see under our clothes."

SEPTEMBER 17
Hildegarde
(d. 1179)

HILDEGARDE WAS A TWELFTH-CENTURY BENEDICTINE Abbess who created a food regimen which, she, as well as many others, believed would lead to spiritual and physical joy.

⁓

One of her more famous elixirs included the following explanations: "For those who are quick-tempered, finding themselves getting upset or angry often, they should quickly warm some wine, add some cold water, drink this down in sufficient quantities until their mood changes. Repeat as needed. The result will be a reduction in their bad moods."

SEPTEMBER 18
Joseph of Cupertino
(d. 1663)

JOSEPH WAS THE SON OF A CARPENTER who sold the family home to pay his debts, forcing his mother to give birth in a stable. From the age of eight, he wandered about his village, aimless and staring into space. He was so absent-minded that his answer to almost everything was "I forgot."

Joseph applied to the Friars Minor Conventuals at seventeen, but was refused because of his inability to carry out simple tasks. He was eventually accepted as a servant with the Franciscans, assigned to work in the stable. His personality changed and a spirit of prayer and penance emerged. This impressed those around him, and Joseph studied to be a priest. He muddled through his studies and almost miraculously was ordained in 1628. He still had little knowledge, but received the gift of spiritual discernment that allowed him to resolve intricate situations.

~

His life became a series of visions and ecstasies (including levitating and floating) which could be triggered at the sound of a church bell, church music, mention of the name of God, as well as any event in the life of Christ. Only the voice of his superior could bring him from his trances. This phenomenon was disturbing to the general public of the time, so Joseph was kept from any public participation in religious ceremonies for thirty-five years.

Joseph is reported to have had a keen sense of insight into what was in people's minds. To people of good conscience, he said: "I don't like scruples or melancholy; let your intentions be the right ones, then don't be afraid."

He often thwarted assassination attempts and, in one case, the poisoning of a king as he pounced on a woman who had prepared a poison vial.

He is known for his advice to many of those who sought absolution: "Go home, wash your face!"

SEPTEMBER 19
Emily de Rodat
(d. 1852)

EMILY DE RODAT STARTED, near Rodez, a convent that later grew into the religious Congregation of the Holy Family.

~

Emily had a gift for amusing remarks. She once said: "There are some people who are not good for a convent, but a convent is good for them; they would be lost in the world, and they don't do much good in a convent—but at least they are kept out of mischief."

Thomas of Villanova

(d. 1555)

THE SON OF A MILLER, he received a good education, becoming a professor of arts, logic, and philosophy. Joining the Augustinians, he was ordained in 1518. He sent the first Augustinians to the New World.

~

Thomas was known as a simple man, one who had great contempt for worldly vanities. Once appointed archbishop, he refused to change his way of dressing, preferring to continue wearing his poor clothing. His old, ragged clothes irritated his canons, who thought it unbecoming to his dignity to be dressed like a pauper. He remarked: "What does a poor friar like me want with such expensive clothes and furniture?" The only concession they wrung from him was that he would wear a silken cap instead of his dirty woolen one. He put this new cap on, saying: "God can see under my garments. He looks as well through wool as silk."

Thomas was a man of unequaled generosity—donating all of his pension to the poor for the welfare of his flock. No single young women in his diocese ever married without a dowry, no orphan failed to have a home, no widow went hungry. He took his charity "on the road," engaging great lords and noblemen to show their greatness and wealth, not through festivities and conspicuous consumption, but by becoming fathers to their vassals. He told them: "Be richer in mercy and charity than in earthly possessions." He would ask them: "Answer me, sinner, what can you buy with your money that is better or more necessary than the redemption of your sins?" At other times, he would tell them: "If you want God to hear your prayers, you must hear the voices of the poor. If you want God to grant you favors, you must grant the wishes of the poor before they even ask."

SEPTEMBER 23
Clare of Assisi
(d. 1253)

BORN INTO A WELL-TO-DO FAMILY, Clare became a close friend of Francis of Assisi after she head him speak and realized that she and he thought alike about spiritual matters. In 1212, after being presented with a special palm on Palm Sunday, she ran away from the family villa to become a religious under Francis. Clare founded the Order of Poor Ladies (the Poor Clares) in San Damiano, and led them for over forty years, making further foundations throughout Europe. It is said that everywhere the Franciscans went, so followed the Poor Clares. Later, she assisted her own mother and sister in joining the cloistered life. Later when she was too ill to attend Mass, an image of the services would project itself on her wall—hence, she is cited as the patroness of television.

~

Pope Gregory IX felt that Clare and her religious had gone too far in their observance of the rule of poverty and tried to impress upon them the need to make provisions for the future—what we might call the "what ifs" (what if we have a famine, what if there is a flood, or a drought). Clare firmly refused. The pope, thinking that she refused because she was afraid to violate her vow of strict poverty, offered to absolve her from it. Clare's reply: "Holy Father, I crave for absolution from my sins, but I do not want to be absolved from my obligation to follow Christ."

Albert of Jerusalem
(d. 1215)

AN ITALIAN WHO BECAME A PRIEST, then bishop of Bobbio and bishop of Vercelli, Albert was instrumental in mediating disputes between the pope and others, especially the Emperor. For this, he was named papal legate to Italy. Co-founder of the Carmelite Friars, he created their rule as an adaptation of one devised by Saint Borcard. He was named patriarch of Jerusalem in 1205, a position that led to conflict with the Muslims and his own martyrdom some ten years later. Summoned, because of his expertise in such matters, to attend the Lateran Council, he was assassinated at the hands of a disgruntled hospital worker whom he had been forced to fire.

~

The Carmelite Rule states that it is basic for a Carmelite to "live a life of allegiance to Christ...pure in heart, stout in conscience...answering to the service of the Master" by

- developing a contemplative dimension in life through an open dialogue with God
- living full of charity
- meditating day and night on the Word of God
- praying alone or with others several times a day
- celebrating the Eucharist daily
- doing manual work
- self-purification of all traces of evil
- living in poverty, placing all personal good in common
- loving the Church and all people
- conforming their will to that of God, seeking that will in faith, through dialogue and discernment

Elzear of Sabran

(d. 1323)

A DEVOUT CHRISTIAN, Elzear was married to the kind and beautiful Delphine, both of whom were devoted to the love of God. Having the same goodness of heart, they consecrated themselves to taking care of the poor.

~

Early in their married life, Elzear set up the following rules for his family (including all who lived under his roof), insisting they be strictly observed:

1. Everyone in the household, no matter what their duties, must go to Mass daily.
2. Swearing, cursing, and blasphemy are forbidden—first offense brings the punishment of chastisement, the second, dismissal.
3. Purity in both speech and action will be enforced.
4. Every member of the household will go to confession weekly, take communion at least on major holidays.
5. No person shall be idle. The men will pray to God in the morning first, then do their work. The women shall pray and read in the morning, but do some work in the afternoon.
6. Dice and all games of chance are forbidden.
7. Slander, gossip, and backbiting are forbidden.
8. If a quarrel arises, the apostolic rule will be observed to settle it.
9. A pious conference will occur every evening, everyone in the household will participate.
10. Oppression and injustice to the poor is forbidden.

Vincent de Paul
(d. 1660)

A PEASANT AND HIGHLY INTELLIGENT PERSON, he spent years with the Franciscans before becoming a children's tutor. A priest at the age of twenty, he was taken captive by Turkish pirates and shipped to Tunis and sold into slavery. He was freed in 1607 when he converted his owner to Christianity.

~

He served as a parish priest near Paris where he established a number of benevolent organizations to assist the poor, nurse the ill, and find jobs for the unemployed. Along with Louise de Marillac, he founded the Congregation of the Daughters of Charity. He also instituted the Congregation of Priests of the Mission (the Lazarists). He founded seminaries to train priests for rural parishes and to integrate acts of corporal mercy with those of spiritual mercy.

Vincent was asked the following question after one of his talks: "What did Jesus say when He was on the cross?"

He replied: "Five statements, and not a single one of them expressed impatience."

The superior of the Sisters of Charity asked Vincent: "How can you put on a happy face when you are feeling unhappy?"

He answered: "At the beginning, you must put on a happy face, even if your heart is not joyful. This isn't dishonest because your love for your fellow sisters shines through because of your desire to love them. If you want to please them, that is sufficient to show happiness on your face. That is how virtues are acquired....If everyone always showed their unhappy feelings, you would see some truly incredibly ugly faces!"

After Vincent refused to grant the bishopric of Poitiers to a certain noblewoman's son, she became so enraged that she grabbed a wooden stool and threw it at Vincent, hitting him on the forehead. Wiping the blood from his brow, he said, "Isn't it wonderful to see a mother's love in action?"

On a certain occasion, Vincent de Paul was speaking to a novice Capuchin who was requesting permission to leave the order because he was so absent-minded, especially at vespers. Vincent asked for a more detailed explanation.

The novice replied: All through vespers, all I could think of was hunting rabbits...my dogs...."

Vincent then asked: "During this time when you were daydreaming, did you ever cry out to your dogs? Did anyone hear you?"

He replied: "No."

Then Vincent said: "Not to worry. You are still worthy to be a monk. We all daydream, but remember, what is important is that we keep it to ourselves and don't cry out during our prayers."

Vincent was not a vain person, just the opposite. Early in his life when his father asked him if he was thinking of entering the priesthood, he replied: "Honestly, I am much too ugly for humanity, but God is not as choosy, so I know he will accept me!"

Vincent's characteristic of humility was also shown when he was insulted by the evil-tongued Saint Cyran who, after Vincent refused to accept his advice, said: "You are an idiot. I'm surprised your Order has allowed you to be its superior." In a lighthearted way, Vincent replied: "You aren't as surprised as I am, for I am even more of an idiot than you think I am!"

About dealing with the devil, Vincent said: "The most powerful weapon we have against the devil is humility—he doesn't know how to use it, nor can he defend himself against it."

SEPTEMBER 28

Faustus of Riez

(d. 490)

FAUSTUS, THE BISHOP OF RIEZ, was one of the most influential bishops of his day.

～

Faustus was often consulted on questions of repentance. Almost always, his reply included the following phrase: "Naked faith, without any merit, is empty, self-serving, and vain."

SEPTEMBER 30

Jerome

(d. 419)

BORN INTO A PAGAN FAMILY, Jerome became a lawyer and then converted to Christianity. He lived for a number of years in the Syrian desert as a hermit. Here occurred the legendary event where Jerome took a thorn out of a lion's paw for which the animal stayed at his side to protect him while he was in the desert. This story accounts for the depiction of Jerome surrounded by lions.

～

Jerome was commissioned by Pope Damasus to revise the Latin text of the Bible resulting, some thirty years later, in the Vulgate translation. He returned to live out his remaining years in desert solitude during which time he continued to write, catalog, and translate religious documents.

About long fasts, Jerome said: "They displease me greatly for I find that the ass that is tired along the road from too long a fast will seek repose at any cost."

It was said of him: "What Jerome is ignorant of, no man has ever known."

About mortification, Jerome said: "The measure of our advancement in the spiritual life is taken from our progress in our mortifications; the greater our mortifications, the closer we are to perfection."

October

~

OCTOBER 1
Thérèse of Lisieux
(d. 1897)

BORN INTO A WORKING-CLASS FRENCH FAMILY, *Thérèse was accepted by the Carmelites when she was fifteen. Her path to God, which she called "The Little Way," one of simplicity, love, and trust, has led many to God. At the request of her superior, and against her own personal desires, she wrote her autobiography,* The Story of a Soul. *She was declared a Doctor of the Church in 1997.*

~

On social class, she said: "True greatness is found in someone's soul, not in their social standing or position."

Thérèse believed in being grateful, saying: "Gratitude is what pleases God the most….If you are grateful for what He grants you, you will receive His blessings tenfold."

About the need to be right, she said: "If it is your goal to always be right in everything, your soul will suffer…even if you are truly right. God is the only One who is always right. He is the only judge….You are just his emissary of peace."

On humility: "We are too little to be able to always rise above difficulties. Well, then, let us pass beneath them."

On going directly to the source: "I felt that talking to God was much better than talking about him."

On finding happiness: "Happiness is not to be found in things...only in the secret places of the soul. You can just as well have it in prison as in a palace."

On the nature of God's love: "As the sun shines on all things on earth in the same way, yet as if each is separate, that is how God's love is for each of us, the same yet unique."

On God as Father: "I think children give as much pleasure to their parents asleep as they do when they are awake. That is why I am no longer upset when I fall asleep when I am praying."

On doing the will of God: "Children don't work for a place in their parents' hearts. If they're good, it's to please their parents. In the same way, we shouldn't work towards being saints, but to please God."

On the desire for sainthood: "I knew that if I always wanted to be a saint, it's because God wants that goal for me and for all of us. He wouldn't let me have that desire if I couldn't attain it, even though I am so small. We can all aspire to sainthood."

On failure: "My last recourse before certain defeat in a struggle is to walk away from the fight....It is better not to expose yourself to it when that outcome is a certainty."

On how to pray: "I pray like a child, simply telling God what is on my mind....He guides me and always understands. Prayer is a burst of love, a look to heaven and a cry of thanks and love in both good times and bad. It bursts my soul open, uniting me with Jesus."

On chastizing effectively: "For punishment to be effective it must be costly for the one who is being punished and carry no malice on the part of the giver."

On rewards: "Justice means not only strictness in levying punishment, but a recognition of good intent and rewarding virtues."

On the power of Jesus: "Alone, I am zero. When I think of zero…I realize that by itself, it has no value, but placed next to a number, it can have great power, provided that it is on the right side, after that number, not in front of it. It is like that for us with Jesus, together with him on his right, we have all of the power in the world."

OCTOBER 2
Leodegar
(d. 678)

BENEDICTINE ABBOT OF THE MONASTERY of Saint Maxentius, and bishop of Autun, Leodegar helped Queen Bathildis when she served as regent for her son Clotaire III. His place at court brought him the enmity of the tyrant Ebroin who had him blinded, imprisoned, and finally beheaded.

～

Leodegar once said: "If monks were what they ought be their prayers would preserve the world from calamities."

OCTOBER 3

Columba Marmion

(d. 1923)

SON OF AN IRISH FATHER AND A FRENCH MOTHER, *Columba was born in Dublin, studied in Rome, and was ordained there in 1881. Following several years as a parish priest, he entered a Benedictine abbey in Belgium at Maredsous. He was elected abbot in 1909—a position he held for the rest of his life. During his time as abbot, Maredsous became a center for spiritual thought. Columba is especially known for his spiritual writings and for skills as a retreat director. It has been said that reading one of Dom Columba's books makes one "touch the face of God."*

~

About the star of Christmas, Dom Columba said: "The star is the symbol of the inward illumination that enlightens souls in order to call them to God."

OCTOBER 4

Francis of Assisi

(d. 1226)

SON OF A RICH MERCHANT, *Francis had a colorful youth. During an imprisonment, he had a mystical experience during which Christ told him to leave his worldly life. When he was released, Francis changed his life and ways. Taking the Gospel as the rule for his life, he dressed in rough garments, begged for food, and preached purity and penance. He visited the sick and preached in the streets, accepting all people as his brothers and sisters.*

To extend his mission, he founded the Franciscans in 1209.

In 1212, with Clare of Assisi, he founded the Poor Clares. He gave up the leadership of the Franciscans in 1221. In 1224, during meditation, he received the stigmata, which periodically bled during the last two years of his life.

~

Saint Francis and a fellow brother found themselves before a Sultan in Egypt in 1219. The Sultan decided that he wished to put Francis's Christianity to the test. Spreading a rug decorated with Christian crosses on the ground, he said to his assistants: "Bring this man who professes to be a Christian to me. If he steps on the crosses, we will say that he has insulted his Lord. If he refuses, we will tell him that he has insulted us."

Francis was called in. He crossed the rug from one end to the other and approached the Sultan. The Sultan then remarked: "You Christians, you worship the cross as a sacred sign, yet you have trampled on it."

Francis replied: "Don't you know that we also crucified thieves with the Lord? We have the true cross and worship it. To you, he has left the thieves' cross—that is why I didn't hesitate to walk on the symbols of bandits."

One day Francis went to see the bishop of Imola to ask permission to preach in his diocese. The bishop curtly replied: "My dear Brother, I preach to my people, that is sufficient."

Francis bowed his head and politely took his leave.

An hour later, Francis returned. The bishop asked: "What do you want now? What permission do you want?"

Francis replied: "Lord, when a father sends his son out one door, he must come back and reenter by another."

Francis's humility so touched the bishop that he and his companions were granted the requested permission.

Francis wanted his followers to have some humor added to their piety and told them: "Leave sadness to the devil, for he indeed has a reason to be sad."

Francis was incensed with the way the papacy of his time had become so corrupt. For his part the pope of the time was incensed that a mere brother would dare to comment about his sins. He was so angered by Francis's appearance before him that he ordered him back to the "pigsty." Francis obeyed and then returned to the pope's side, asking to speak to him about his personal lifestyle. The pope was now enraged, sending the "madman" away after he had left muddy tracks on his magnificent carpets. Francis refused to budge, stating that he had indeed done what the pontiff had requested and gone to the pigsty. The Holy Father was hopping mad. Francis was again ordered to exit, but he refused to move. Finally, Pope Innocent calmed down a little, saying: "Go and get cleaned up, come back tomorrow, and I will hear what you have to say." As a mark of respect, Francis bowed to kiss the pontiff's feet but, in an effort to avoid him, the pope lurched backwards, almost falling in the process. As he was exiting, the pontiff asked Francis: "How did you find a pigsty?" The reply came: "I went behind your stables, in the back of the palace."

"How did you know where to look?" he shot back.

"As I came through the city, your stables were pointed out to me and I smelled the sty. And I thought to myself, the pope's pigs smell exactly the same as peasants's pigs."

Francis's monks asked him about whether they should eat meat on the Friday of the following week, since it was also Christmas day. Francis replied: "Why not eat meat on the day the Word was made flesh?"

On one of his trips to Rome, Francis stayed at the residence of Cardinal Leo. During the visit, Francis was beaten severely by devils. Rather than get overexcited, Francis simply stated: "This is my punishment for consorting with cardinals."

Francis said this on the happiness of sharing: "Jesus is happy to accompany us, just as the truth is happy to be spoken, life is to be lived, as a light is to be lit, as love is to be loved, as joy is to be shared, and as peace is to be spread to others."

OCTOBER 5
Francis Xavier Seelos
(d. 1867)

NAMED FOR SAINT FRANCIS XAVIER, he wanted to be a priest from an early age and often claimed that he would be just like his namesake. Of German origin, his studies were in the fields of philosophy and theology. He entered the seminary in 1842, joining the Congregation of the Most Holy Redeemer (the Redemptorists). Sensing a calling to go to assist German immigrants in America, he left the seminary and arrived in New York in 1843. Ordained in Baltimore in 1844, he worked in Pittsburgh as the assistant pastor and student of Saint John Neumann.

Francis led a simple life and was always available to those in need. He worked on the Redemptorist mission team, was appointed to numerous parishes, and served as a seminary teacher. During the American Civil War, he met with President Lincoln and successfully secured an exemption from service for seminarians. Finally, moving to New Orleans in 1866, where he heard his services would be needed for an influx of German immigrants, he died the following year while caring for victims of yellow fever.

~

Father Seelos was known for his cheerfulness and humor, which he used as an instrument for evangelization. He usually saw the humor in life situations and pointed that out to others as a means of celebrating our little idiosyncracies. He stated that he thought humor was a means to help someone grow in charity—his "holy hilarity," as some call it. Numerous stories abound about his gentle, upbeat look at life.

On one occasion, later in his life, Father was the prefect of students at the Redemptorist seminary in Maryland. Hearing that the students had formed a laughing society, he was eager to join. To belong, each member would have to tell a joke upon request, but no one was allowed to laugh at it until all members were consulted to decide if it was funny—if so decided, then members were allowed to laugh when the signal was given, but then they had to stop laughing when told to do so. If this rule wasn't followed, a prescribed penance was assigned. It is said that Father Seelos often had to leave the room after a joke was told because he couldn't stop laughing and couldn't afford the time for any more penances.

Even on his deathbed, Father Seelos had a sense of humor. In one of his less delirious moments caused by the fatal yellow fever—he was asked if he had anything to say, before he died, to his brothers and sisters back home in Germany, with respect to his family's inheritance. Considering the poverty of his younger years, he replied: "Nothing at all. Before I came to America, we arranged all of that in a fraternal way—I get nothing and they also get nothing!

Bruno

(d. 1101)

BORN AT COLOGNE, Bruno studied at Reims and Paris. He was appointed chancellor of the diocese of Reims, but later, along with six others, went to the Le Grande Chartreuse, from which the order he founded (the Carthusians) evolved. Pope Urban II sent for Bruno to enter his service in Rome. While there, he managed to start another monastery, this one in Calabria. He was finally allowed to retire there.

～

In one of the letters Bruno wrote to a friend, he stated: "Those who are called to the eremetical life must have a happy soul, for nothing is more destructive than sadness."

OCTOBER 9

John Leonardi

(d. 1609)

JOHN SERVED AS A PHARMACIST'S APPRENTICE while he studied for the priesthood, being ordained in 1571. Along with a group of laymen and priests, John founded the Institute of Clerks Regular of the Mother of God. Their order was dedicated to education, reform of the clergy, and the works of mercy. He is considered one of the founders of the college in Rome that trains priests for foreign missions. He died of the plague transmitted to him during visits to the sick.

～

An implementer of the reforms of the Council of Trent, John wrote to Pope Paul V that those who undertook the reform of people's morals should "place themselves in the sight of the people as mirrors of all the virtues, like lamps set on a stand to give light by their integrity of life and example…thus they will draw them gently to reform rather than compel them, and there will not be required of the body what is not found in the head."

OCTOBER 10

Francis Borgia
(d. 1572)

BORN IN SPAIN *Francis was the son of the duke of Gandia. For ten years (from 1528), Francis, was in the service of Emperor Charles V as an adviser. When Charles's empress died, Francis witnessed the decomposing body of the woman who had been such a great beauty in her lifetime. This jolted him and, thereafter, he devoted himself to prayer. In 1543, his father died and Francis inherited his titles and estates. Finding himself out of favor with the court, Francis retired to his estates, founding a monastery, setting up a college of theology, and restoring a hospital. In 1546, Francis's wife died, leaving eight children of whom the youngest was eight years old.*

Shortly after the death of Francis's wife, a message was sent to Saint Ignatius in Rome that Francis wished to become a Jesuit. Ignatius advised him to wait until he made arrangements for the well-being of his children and had finished a doctorate in theology. When Francis was called back to court, he quickly wrote to Ignatius, asking him to let him make his profession privately. Francis left for Rome in August 1550, made his profession, and returned to Spain within four months. Retiring to a hermitage, Francis shaved his head and beard, donned clerical robes, and was ordained a priest in 1551.

~

He did all he could to make others forget his upper-class origins, but his abilities could not be hidden. His preaching drew huge crowds in Spain and Portugal. He went through the villages with a bell, calling the children and adults to catechism. In 1554, Ignatius appointed Francis provincial for Spain and the Indies. In this office, Francis popularized the then little-known Jesuits, founding numerous houses and colleges, and attracting many good recruits. Four years later, Francis was unanimously elected father general of the Jesuits. The order made great progress during his seven-year rule; he has, indeed, been called its second founder. On a diplomatic mission for the pope, Francis became so ill that he was sent back to Rome where he died two days later.

Francis was very severe on himself after joining the Jesuits. He had been a very corpulent man until his girth was noticeably trimmed by his fasting and other mortifications. He signed himself "Francis the Sinner," until Ignatius ordered him not to do so.

On his deathbed, Francis pronounced a blessing on each of his children and grandchildren. When he was no longer able to speak, a painter was sent to his bedside to record his appearance. Francis expressed his displeasure with this vanity and turned his face away so that nothing could be done.

Many were surprised by Francis's choice of the Jesuits, since they were a new, young order. In answer to his refusal to accept the habit of an older, more established order, he replied: "Age is no guarantee of goodness.

Edwin

(d. 633)

KING OF NORTHUMBRIA, Edwin became a convert to Christianity at Easter in 627. He fell in battle fighting against the pagan Welsh.

∼

Edwin is quoted as having said, in response to his desire for peace and the reasons for his conversion: "Life is like the flight of the sparrow when he flies through the warm dining room on a winter's day. He flies in one door out the other, from the dark and cold of the winter outside to the warmth and light indoors….If we are not careful, he will return to the darkness and cold of the winter…but if we increase his knowledge of the warmth offered inside, he will stay. It is the same with Christianity."

Edward the Confessor

(d. 1066)

THE SON OF KING ETHELRED II who was unseated by a Danish invasion, he and his brother were sent to Denmark to be quietly killed, but were saved by an officer who sent them to Sweden, then to Hungary, where they were raised by the king to return at a later date. Edward gained the reputation of being just and worthy of the throne and was given public support. He ascended to the throne in 1042. During this time, he was generous to the poor, and was known for his piety and love of God.

∼

A romantic account of Edward is told in this unsubstantiated story: Easter time 1053 saw Edward dining with Earl Godwin when Edward saved Godwin from certain disaster because of an accident involving a servant falling with his hands full. Godwin commented: "One brother helping another." To this, Edward replied, "I once had a brother who would have helped me had you not killed him." Godwin replied, "You have accused me of this crime of killing your brother, Alfred, many times over the years. I now call God as a witness to my innocence. If I am not innocent, may this piece of bread choke me to death." Godwin then proceeded to take the piece of bread from the table and place it in his mouth. The bread stuck in his throat almost immediately, choking him to death.

OCTOBER 15
Teresa of Ávila
(d. 1582)

THE DAUGHTER OF A SPANISH NOBLE, she grew up interested in the saints' lives. She was schooled at home because she had been handicapped at a young age, but was cured after she prayed to Saint Joseph. Her mother died when she was twelve, and Teresa prayed to Our Lady to be her replacement. Because of family opposition, she secretly left home at the age of seventeen to become a Carmelite.

She was gifted with visions, which were examined and pronounced genuine. Considering her religious order to be too lax, she founded a reformed convent and several other houses. She was a mystical writer and proclaimed a Doctor of the Church in 1970.

~

While on one of her many trips, among many other disasters, Teresa fell and injured her leg. She promptly turned to God and said: "Lord, you couldn't have picked a worse time for this to happen—haven't I had enough problems?"

The Lord replied: "Don't you realize that this is how I treat my friends?"

Teresa retorted: "If this is how you treat your friends, it's no wonder you don't have very many."

One day, Teresa was invited to dine with a notable religious Brother. They were served partridge (quite a delicacy). A servant was quite amazed and almost insulted to see a religious who was as famous as she for her minimalist attitude agree to share such a meal. In answer to her comments, Teresa replied: "My dear young woman, remember this, when there are partridges, we eat partridges, when it is time for penance, we do penance. Everything in its own time."

Teresa said, perhaps tongue in cheek: "From silly devotions, and somber, serious, sullen saints, save us, O Lord. Lord, hear our prayer."

Teresa of Ávila spent a great deal of time traveling around Spain from convent to convent. She loved God and her friends with enthusiastic zeal. She said: "I have no defense against affection. I could be bribed with a sardine."

Teresa decided to stay overnight on All Saints' Day (1570) at Salamanca, where she had just established a monastery. The only room that was available was with a sister in a room from which students had been expelled and in which other unpleasant things had been known to happen. The sister was truly afraid, furtively glancing in all directions, she asked: "Mother, what would you do if I died and left you all alone here?" In a lively manner, Teresa replied: "Sister, if that happens, I will tend to what I have to do, but for now, let me get some sleep."

In a preface to one of her books, Teresa comments: "I must warn my readers that since I have such a poor memory, many things that should have been included have been left out—and my poor judgment may have led me to include things that would have been better left out."

A friend countered rumors that Teresa had read the Bible, especially the Song of Songs with this anecdote: "In Toledo, a young lady applied for admission to Teresa's convent, saying she owned a Bible and would bring it with her. Teresa responded as a saint should: 'Bible, daughter? We want neither you, nor your Bible. We are ignorant women who only know how to spin and follow orders.'"

Teresa and John of the Cross were sometimes on the opposite sides of a paradox as explained in this story. John, when offered some rather delicious looking grapes, said: "If someone thought about God's justice, he would never eat these." Teresa quickly retorted: "But if that same person thought of his goodness, he wouldn't stop eating them."

Teresa's point of view on good humor: "A sad nun is a bad nun....I am more afraid of one unhappy sister than a crowd of evil spirits....What would happen if we hid what little sense of humor we had? Let each of us humbly use this to cheer others."

When Teresa was questioned about how she could found so many convents with so little money, she replied: "Teresa and a couple of pennies is nothing, but Teresa, a couple of pennies, and God, that is everything one needs."

Gerard Majella
(d. 1755)

THE SON OF A POOR TAILOR who died when Gerard was twelve, he initially joined the Redemptorists as a lay brother. Gerard died at the age of twenty-nine.

~

When Gerard was facing his final illness, he had this note posted on his sick-room door: "Here the will of God is done, as God wills, and as long as he wills it."

Gerard had an extraordinary devotion to the Blessed Sacrament. Once, with the few cents he had left, he bought some flowers. Going up the steps of the altar of the Most Blessed Sacrament, he placed them at the foot of the tabernacle and said: "Lord, you see, I have thought of you, now it's your turn to think of me."

Margaret Mary Alocoque
(d. 1690)

MARGARET MARY, A VISITATION NUN, had a difficult religious life for its very constitution declares that "no Visitation nun must be extraordinary, except through being ordinary." The Lord appeared to her on numerous occasions, yet, when discussing these visits with her superior, she was punished, and the superior "mortified and humiliated her with all of her might ...not allowing her to do any of the things the Lord asked of her." It was an uphill battle, won, in large part, through the efforts of her confessor, Claude de la Colombière.

One of the most famous series of these visions was the one during which the practice of first Fridays came to be. Kneeling before the Blessed Sacrament, Margaret Mary at once felt she was "invested" by the presence of the Lord. He told her that the love of his Sacred Heart must be spread throughout the world through her as his instrument. His heart was then united with her own, and then he returned it to her, burning with the desire to spread devotion to his Sacred Heart. During the eighteen months of this type of exchange, the devotion to, and symbolism of, the Sacred Heart was explained to Margaret Mary. But another special devotion was requested by Our Lord: frequent Communion must be practiced, especially on the first Friday of every month. Thus was instituted the practices of the First Fridays and the feast of the Sacred Heart.

OCTOBER 17
Richard Gwyn
(d. 1584)

ALSO KNOWN AS RICHARD WHITE, this convert from Protestantism was born in Wales. He married, became a schoolteacher, and was imprisoned for four years before he was executed.

Richard cheerfully thwarted all attempts at reconverting him: Arrested, Richard was brought before a magistrate, who offered him release if he converted back to Protestantism. He refused and was returned to jail in chains. Later he was forcibly taken to a service in a Protestant church, where he interrupted everyone by persistently rattling his chains. Next he was put in the stocks where he was visited by a steady stream of Protestant ministers. One of these ministers, endowed with the characteristic red nose of a drinker, stated that he had the power of the keys to the kingdom of God to the same extent as did Saint Peter. Gwyn retorted: "It seems to me that the only keys you seem to have in your pocket are the ones to the tavern."

OCTOBER 19

Peter of Alcántara
(d. 1562)

BORN IN SPAIN, Peter joined the Franciscans and after ordination instituted a more severe form of the Franciscan rule. He is one of the great Spanish mystics, confessor of Teresa of Ávila who said of him that his penances had made him look as if "he had been made of the roots of trees."

After having been responsible for the friary's refectory for six months, the friars questioned Peter on his decision not to give them any fruit during that period of time. His answer: "I hadn't seen any"; in fact, he hadn't lifted his eyes from the floor once during that time—the fruit was hanging from the ceiling.

A few years later, his austerities took on rather unusual characteristics. Even as a priest and later, as superior, setting the strictest example for others, Peter refused to have the extravagance of more than one habit or coat. So, when washing day came around, he would give his garments to be washed and then find himself a warm, secluded spot in the garden, waiting there, with nothing on, until the clothes were dry.

When people were saddened about the evils of the world, Peter would reply: "The remedy is simple. You and I must first be what we ought to be; then we shall have cured what concerns ourselves. Let each one do the same, and all will be well. The trouble is that we all talk of reforming others without ever reforming ourselves."

OCTOBER 21
Margaret Clitherow
(d. 1586)

MARGARET WAS THE DAUGHTER of a candlemaker and had been reared as a Protestant. People who knew Margaret describe her as well-liked, attractive, merry, and witty. "Everyone loved her and would run to her for help, comfort, and counsel in distress."

Three years after her marriage to a Protestant, Margaret became a Catholic. She was an active, outspoken Catholic and was imprisoned for two years for failure to attend the parish church. She was confined in a filthy, cold cell, given the poorest prison fare, and separated from her family, yet she herself refers to this time as "happy and profitable."

In a specially built room she hid priests who sought refuge from penal laws, and her home became one of the most important hiding places of the time. In 1584, she was confined to her home for a year and a half, apparently for sending her eldest son to Douai in France to be educated. Her husband remained silent about her activities, and his children were interrogated and gave nothing away. However, a Flemish student broke down under threats and revealed the secret hiding place for priests. Accused of a capital offense, Margaret was taken to prison. She was tried, convicted, and sentenced to be pressed to death.

At the age of thirty, Margaret went to her death smiling, carrying over her arm a long white robe; her shroud, which she had made in prison. She had sent her hat to her husband "in sign of her loving duty to him as to her head," and her shoes and stockings to her daughter, that she should follow in her steps.

One of Margaret's only regrets was her failure to bring her Protestant husband back to the true faith. She perhaps had discerned the reason for his refusal: "He hath too much; he cannot lift up his head to God for the weight of his goods."

OCTOBER 23

Ignatius of Constantinople
(d. 877)

THE SON OF THE BYZANTINE EMPEROR, Ignatius was turned into a eunuch by his uncle (so he would not claim the family fortune, the throne, or provide heirs) and was exiled to a monastery. He eventually became a priest and then patriarch of Constantinople. He fought a battle against corruption, both in the secular as well as religious arenas. Because he had refused to soften his strict requirements and grant absolution to the incestuous regent for the emperor, he was exiled for ten years, only to return at a later date in triumph.

Ignatius said about death of the body: "My body has already been marred—I have died to myself and I spend each day learning to die more perfectly."

Ignatius's verdict on his uncle's castration of him and his brother: "My uncle has done me a great service, for now, as I curb my sensual desires and regulate those passions, I enjoy an inner peace that the entire world can't take away from me."

OCTOBER 27
Contardo Ferrini
(d. 1902)

AN ITALIAN BY BIRTH, Contardo took degrees in civil and canon law. Afterwards he taught at Italian universities, becoming involved in Christian politics and service to the poor. A devout lay Catholic, Contardo was a Franciscan tertiary and a member of the Saint Vincent de Paul Society. He died of typhoid fever.

~

Having taken a secret vow of celibacy, Contardo constantly had friends who were trying to find a wife for him. One friend used the following arguments when recommending an eligible young woman to him: "Well, when her father dies...she will have so much money. When her mother dies, so much more... and when her uncle dies...." Contardo cut in: "Stop. I can't think. There are too many corpses."

Contardo was known for his prayerful love of nature: "Nature lives by the breath of God's omnipotence, smiles in its joy of him, hides from his wrath—yet greets him, eternally young, with the smile of its own youth."

Narcissus of Jerusalem

(d. 215)

APPOINTED BISHOP OF JERUSALEM at the age of eighty, Narcissus was an attendee at a council in Palestine to discuss the proper way of deciding the date of Easter. He was a strict upholder of Church law and, in the face of slanderous attacks, retired to live a life of solitude.

~

Eusebius tells of the many miracles Narcissus worked during his lifetime. Here is one: On Easter eve, it was noticed that the supply of oil for the church's lamps had run out since the deacons had forgotten to order a sufficient supply. Narcissus told his deacons to fill the lamps with water. To the amazement of all who were present, after prayers, the water had miraculously been changed into oil.

In spite of his advanced age when he became the bishop, Narcissus was not weak. Narcissus is reputed to have accused three men of perjury. One of the men replied: "May I be burned alive if I am lying." The second said: "May I be stricken with leprosy if I am lying." The third chimed in, "May I go blind if I am lying." Within a matter of days, the first man died with his entire family in a house fire. The second died of leprosy. And the third was so terrified that he would go blind he confessed to the crime of which he was accused. It is said that he cried so many tears of repentance that he did indeed go blind.

Alonso Rodriguez

(d. 1617)

BORN IN SPAIN, Alonso became a merchant and married, but lost his wife and children within the space of three years. He joined the Jesuits as a lay brother at the age of forty-four and served for many years as a doorkeeper of a college.

~

Alonso proves Mother Teresa's saying that small things done with great love is what all Christians are called to do. Daily, he prayed to more than twenty saints, confessors, martyrs and Church Fathers.

It is said that Alonso was perhaps a little mad, for when he was told to finish his plate completely, he took his utensils and did just that, explaining that he had taken a vow of obedience and that was that.

Alonso's faith was uncomplicated and simple, as was his advice: "To try to know oneself is the foundation of everything. He who knows himself despises himself, while he who does not know himself is pulled up."

November

NOVEMBER 1
Salaun
(d. 1358)

A POOR BEGGAR of Brittany who went from door to door asking for alms, Salaun was known for his reverence for the Blessed Virgin. When knocking at doors, or meeting someone on the road, he would cry: "O Lady Virgin Mary, Salaun would like some bread to eat." His bizarre activities, such as sleeping in trees, made Salaun a "fool for Christ."

When Salaun died and was buried in his local churchyard, a pure white lily grew out of his grave—the petals were inscribed with his famous words: "O Lady Virgin Mary." The lily remained in flower for six full weeks. Neighbors, curious as to the origin of the flower, dug up his grave and found that the lily was growing directly from the dead man's mouth.

Martin de Porres

(d. 1639)

THE ILLEGITIMATE SON of a Spanish nobleman and a freed slave in Peru, he grew up in poverty, learning the rudiments of medicine from a surgeon/barber. At eleven, he became a servant for the Dominicans, later appointed collector of alms, a job at which he was quite successful. Placed in charge of the infirmary, he was known for his tender care of the ill as well as miraculous cures. Martin is the first black saint of the Americas.

~

Martin could joke with the best of them, insisting that sheep knew the true meaning of charity since they always gave their extra coat to the poor.

He was known as "Martin the Charitable" since he did not look down on or refuse care to blacks, mulattos, or the poor, stating: "We are all God's children, created in his image."

Martin's sympathetic care extended to animals. Pictures show him with a basket collecting mice from the cubbyholes of the church. It is said that he would take them outside, give them food, and tell them not to harm the crops or go back to the churches.

Charles Borromeo

(d. 1584)

BORN INTO A NOBLE ITALIAN FAMILY, Charles was a lawyer at the age of twenty-one, a cardinal at twenty-two, and the archbishop of Milan at twenty-four. He spent his entire life in service to others. Charles strenuously enforced the decrees of the Council of Trent and fought to repair the damage caused by Martin Luther and founded schools for the poor, seminaries, and hospitals. It is believed that he was the first to institute children's Sunday schools.

~

Recreation and leisure time are as important to the saints as anyone else. One day, Charles was playing pool when a friend asked: "What would you do right this minute if someone came in and told you that you would die in fifteen minutes?" Pausing only a heartbeat, Charles replied: "I'd probably continue to play pool."

Later in his life, when Charles was a cardinal, it came time to elect a successor to Pius V. In poor health, and against his doctors' advice, Charles decided to go to Rome to participate in the conclave, with one concession—that he bring along a number of varied medicines, serums, and potions. When his journey reached about the midway point, the caravan had to ford across a stream. To the horror of other travelers, the mule carrying the cardinal's medicines fell into the water, destroying all of them. Charles chuckled, saying: "This is a sign from heaven—I no longer need any medicine."

Charles practiced many austerities, but very discreetly. When someone would have a bed warmer placed in his bed for him, Charles would refuse this luxury stating: "The best way not to find a bed so cold is to make sure that you are colder than the bed is."

Charles was a reformer, and not well-liked by many of those under his supervision. As cardinal, Charles's changes were seen as just that, changes, and resisted very fervently, to the point that many attempts were made on his life. In 1569, a guard was posted at his door to protect his life and permit him to celebrate Mass in safety. Three members of a particular religious order which had few members but great wealth, formulated a plot to kill the cardinal. One of three would-be assassins agreed to do the deed for forty pieces of gold. One evening, as Charles was at evening prayers, singing the final words of a hymn, he was shot. Upon closer investigation, it was discovered that it was a flesh wound and Charles was only bruised. Retiring to a monastery to recover for a few days, Charles later returned to an active public life—never to sing that hymn ever again.

NOVEMBER 6
Christina Bruzo
(d. 1312)

BORN IN THE VILLAGE OF STOMMELN, *not far from Cologne, Germany, Christine's father was a farmer. It appears, from all reports, Christine led a life filled with many inexplicable events. These events appear to have begun at the age of five when she began having visions of Christ as a child. At the age of eleven, she began to read the psalter, although it was reported that she could neither read nor write. After her parents arranged a marriage for her at the age of twelve, she ran off to a convent where she could live a life of poverty and penance.*

There she received the stigmata on her hands and feet, the marks of the crown of thorns on her head, as well as the wounds in her side. Many disbelieved her and even though there were eyewitnesses to these phenomena, the members of her religious order thought she was mentally ill and sent her home.

Once home, her own parish priest took her into his house where she lived a pious life, maintaining her religious habit and keeping her vows. Testimonials attest to her experiences of divine ecstasies.

A pious young Dominican named Peter of Dacia made Christina's acquaintance and he kept a record of what he saw in connection with her. He tells especially of Christina's attacks by the devil, of her being sunk up to her neck in a mud pit, of Satan fixing hot stones to her body, and of being dragged from her bed and tied to a tree. Many of these events seem almost hallucinatory and fabricated, but Christina's personal virtue is undoubted.

NOVEMBER 7
Willibrord of Utrecht
(d. 739)

APOSTLE OF HOLLAND and first archbishop of Utrecht, Willibrod was blessed with a cheerful and charitable manner. He built churches and founded monasteries in his diocese for both men and women and gradually spread knowledge of the Gospel to his people.

～

Willibrod was very successful in converting many to Christianity, including the son of Radbod, the pagan king, who was just on the point of his own conversion. When Willibrod had Radbod himself in the waters of the baptismal stream, the latter stopped the proceedings and asked his baptizer: "Where are your ancestors' souls?" Expecting the answer to be "in heaven," Radbod was surprised to hear Willibrod's honesty win out and reply—"in hell." "Well then," replied Radbod, as he withdrew himself from the baptismal waters: "I would rather be in hell, celebrating with a race of heroes than in heaven with a pack of beggars."

NOVEMBER 8
Gernad
(d. 934)

AN IRISH HERMIT, Gernad built himself a cell at Kenedor and was instrumental in converting numerous English soldiers during the wars between England and Scotland. These stories are told about Gernad.

~

On one occasion, a wolf which had slain one of Gernad's oxen in order to feed itself and its family, took the oxen's place and finished its plowing duties for the season, until Gernad could get another.

Around the year 934, Gernad was in the process of building a church. He was plagued with many problems—the most pressing was how to get the necessary timber from the highlands down to the construction site. Gernad prayed to find a solution to his problem. The next day, a violent storm diverted the river, which ran next to the site, into another stream, so that the timber could be easily brought down from the forest. His church was built.

NOVEMBER 10
Andrew of Avellino
(1608)

AN ITALIAN PRIEST and ecclesiastical lawyer, Andrew abandoned law because of his horror of losing a case. He entered religious life with the Theatines and became a spiritual director and advisor to Saint Charles Borremeo.

~

A priest asked Andrew: "How long should one remain at the bedside of a sick person?"

He replied: "Always be brief. There are two advantages: if they like you, they will be happy to see you come back. If you are boring, their displeasure will be short."

NOVEMBER 11
Martin of Tours
(d. 397)

BORN OF PAGAN PARENTS, he was raised in Italy. Joining the army at the age of fifteen, he converted to Christianity at eighteen. Later after becoming a priest, he preached throughout France and eventually became the Bishop of Tours.

~

On an occasion when Martin was destroying pagan temples, a man came up behind him with a sword in his hand. Martin bared his chest. Surprised, the man lost his balance, fell backwards, and asked for forgiveness and baptism.

Encountering a beggar while he was on horseback, Martin realized he had nothing to give but the clothes on his back. Unsheathing his sword, he promptly cut his cloak in half, giving it to the beggar. That night, he had a vision of Christ wearing his very cloak.

On his deathbed, some of the priests at his bedside felt that they should turn his body over to give him some relief. Martin stopped them saying: "Brothers, allow me to keep my eyes on heaven rather than earth so that my spirit can set its course in the right direction when it's time for me to leave on my journey to the Lord."

NOVEMBER 13
Brice of Tours
(d. 444)

AN ORPHAN, *rescued and raised by Martin of Tours, Brice was a child with behavioral problems so severe that people believed him to be possessed by the devil. Brice became a priest and, when Martin died, Brice was designated to succeed him. The people of Tours rebelled, forcing Brice to leave town to avoid a stoning. Brice lived a pious life for some thirty years and finally formal investigations cleared him of all wrongdoings. Brice then returned to Tours to assume his rightful place, and the inhabitants, remembering his past, ran him out of town again, appointing another successor. Some ten years later, upon the death of this person, Brice again tried to claim his proper role. This time, he sent word of his exemplary forty years while in exile and he was allowed into Tours to govern the diocese until his death.*

~

It has been said that God has a remarkable sense of humor. He inexplicably takes pleasure in placing two saints side by side who can, under no circumstances, ever get along.

This is a lesson in humility and proof that there are not only many rooms in the Father's house but also many paths one could take.

As a priest, Brice still had great contempt for Martin, the only father he ever knew. When asked how he could put up with Brice, Martin replied: "If Jesus could deal with Judas, I can deal with Brice."

NOVEMBER 16

Agnes of Assisi
(d. 1253)

THE YOUNGER SISTER and first follower of Saint Clare of Assisi, she left home two weeks after Clare to join her. From the very beginning of her religious life, Agnes was distinguished for such an incredible degree of virtue that her companions stated that she had indeed discovered a new road to perfection. In 1221, a group of Benedictine nuns in Monticelli (near Florence) asked to join the Poor Clares, and Saint Francis assigned Agnes as their abbess. She wrote many letters about how much she missed her sister and the other nuns at San Damiano (the original foundation). She was recalled there when Clare was dying. Agnes died just three months later.

~

The family tried to forcefully bring her back, physically dragging her from the monastery, pulling her by the hair, and kicking her repeatedly. Her sister Clare intervened and, suddenly, Agnes' body became so heavy that several knights could not budge her. Her uncle tried to strike her, but he was immediately paralyzed, his arm dropping to his side.

Gertrude the Great

(d. 1302)

As a child of five, Gertrude was offered to God at Helfta, a Benedictine monastery in Saxony. At twenty-five, she began to experience mystical visions of Christ, making her realize that Christ was dwelling within her. Gertrude became known through her writings: Herald of Divine Love *and her* Spiritual Exercises.

∼

Here is Gertrude's vision of Mary: "On the Feast of the Annunciation I saw the heart of the Virgin Mother so bathed by the rivers of grace flowing out of the Blessed Trinity that I understood the privilege Mary has of being the most powerful after God the Father, the most wise after God the Son, and the most kindly after God the Holy Spirit."

In a vision of Christ, Gertrude saw his hand take hers, and heard Christ say to her: "You have licked the dust of my enemies and sucked honey from thorns. Now come back to me, and my divine delights shall be as wine to you."

Hugh of Lincoln

(d. 1200)

THE SON OF THE LORD OF AVALON (FRANCE), his mother died when he was eight. Raised and educated in a convent, he became a monk at fifteen, deacon at nineteen, a Carthusian priest, and the prior of the monastery. In 1175, he became abbot at the first English Carthusian monastery, which was built by King Henry II as part of his penance for the murder of Thomas Becket. Later appointed bishop of Lincoln (England), he had a great reputation for holiness that attracted many people. He denounced the mass persecution of Jews in England, frequently facing armed mobs, forcing them to release their victims. Hugh traveled to France as an ambassador on behalf of King John. His health failed there, and upon his return two months later, he died.

~

Hugh was rather bold and somewhat more forthright when he was called to correct the errors of others. On one occasion when he was riding to a parish for a confirmation, he was flagged down by a farmer who insisted that he be confirmed there and then. Hugh administered his confirmation, but when it came time to give him the customary ritual slap, it was one that would send any "golden gloves" contender to the mat.

Hugh took great pleasure in visiting the leper houses. When an assistant pointed out to him that Saint Martin had cured leprosy by his touch, Hugh answers: "Saint Martin's kiss healed the leper's flesh; but their kiss heals my soul."

Cecilia of Rome

(d. third century)

THE PATRONESS of church music and musicians (because she is purported to have played the music at her own wedding), little is reliably known of her early life. It is believed that she was born into a noble family in Rome and raised a Christian.

She was given in marriage, against her will, to a young pagan nobleman named Valerian.

～

The legend of Cecilia is a well-known and well-loved story, but it is by no means authentic. Here it is in brief: In their wedding chamber, she said to her new husband: "I have an angel of God watching over me. If you even touch me, he will get angry and you will suffer for it. But if you respect my maidenhood, my angel will love you just as he loves me." Her new husband asked to see this angel. Cecilia responded that if he was a believer in the one true and living God, and baptized, he would be able to see him. Impressed by his wife's sincere beliefs, he left and was baptized a Christian the next day. Upon returning from the ceremony, he found his wife standing next to the angel, just as she had promised. The angel then crowned Cecilia with roses and Valerian with lilies. Valerian's brother entered the room during this heavenly coronation and was converted on the spot. From that time on, the two young men dedicated their lives to good works, one of which was the burial of martyred Christians for which they both were arrested, tortured, and beheaded.

Cecilia herself, was brought before the court, judged to be a Christian, and sentenced to death by suffocation in her home. For this particular execution, they stoked her furnace with seven times its normal level of fuel, releasing excessive amounts of steam into her bathroom. This failed to kill her, so a soldier tried to behead her, unsuccessfully striking her neck three times with a sword, leaving her bleeding on the floor of her home. Lingering for three days, crowds of Christians at her side, she finally died.

NOVEMBER 23
Columbanus
(d. 615)

WELL INSTRUCTED FROM CHILDHOOD, Columbanus was said to have been quite handsome, a fact that caused him great personal conflict and forced him constantly to fight temptations. Sometimes headstrong and impetuous, both before and after he became a monk, Columbanus finally was given permission to undertake missionary expeditions at the age of forty.

Setting sail with twelve companions, he first went to Britain, then France. Wherever they went, people were overcome by their humility, patience, modesty, zeal, piety, and education. Many disciples of his simple ways flocked to his side. The numbers forced Columbanus to found monasteries to accommodate them, also writing a rule for their wellbeing. It is said that he prepared for his impending death by retiring to a cave on a mountainside, overlooking a river.

Columbanus's teaching states: "It is better to have a true hour, patiently passed here on earth, than to wake up to pain that comes much too late to do anything about it, and lasts for all time."

About fasting Columbanus said: "It is better to eat one meal, in the evening, than to overstuff the body and suffocate the mind with food." Columbanus goes on to state: "You need to eat, but only once a day—and that, so you have the strength to pray, work in the fields and read Scripture. It is a sin for a monk to not only eat too much, but want to eat more than he needs to fuel his body."

Columbanus composed his own "Irish Rule" as a means of leading his monks on a road to perfection. Therein was a list of standardized penances for those who "strayed" from this path. Some of these penances included the following: six strokes of the whip for

- failing to say grace before meals
- not saying "Amen" after food is blessed
- unnecessary talking at the dinner table
- expressing ownership (as all things were held by the community)
- those who forgot the Sign of the Cross at the table
- those who raised their voices without due reason (due reason equals fire)
- those who coughed during the singing of Psalms at Office (if ill, ask someone else); or
- those who smiled during the recitation of Office

Seeking the advice of a religious woman whom he respected, Columbanus asked her how could he avoid succumbing to the natural call to procreate. Her reply: "Do you think Adam could resist Eve? Was Samson not made weak by Dalila? David was lured by the beauty of Bathsheba? Solomon deceived by the love of all women? And you think you will be able to avoid women on your own, with no help? You must have fallen into a river and hit your head."

Peter of Alexandria

(d. 311)

BISHOP OF ALEXANDRIA, Peter was beheaded by Roman officials acting on the orders of Emperor Maximian. Peter was the last Christian martyr of the Roman persecutions. A model bishop, known for his virtue, Peter composed a set of rules governing the readmittance of those Christians who had left the faith in the face of persecution. These Penitential Canons were seen to be too lax by some of Peter's opponents.

~

Peter's rules soon became part of Eastern church law: "Those who had paid money so as not be molested were not required to do any penance, nor were those who had fled even if others were arrested in their place. Those, however, who pretended to apostatize or who sent pagans to sacrifice in their place were required to do six months of penance. Anyone who voluntarily came forward to denounce himself was not to be disturbed even if his way of acting brought persecution on others. Those who fell through lack of courage without suffering either torture or imprisonment had to do penance for three years."

Leonard of Port Maurice

(d. 1751)

THE SON OF A SEA CAPTAIN, he was placed with an uncle at the age of thirteen to study to be a doctor. Deciding against this career, he was disowned. Continuing his studies at the Jesuit College in Rome, he joined the Franciscans of the Strict Observance in 1697 and was ordained in 1703. He wanted to become a missionary to China, but a bleeding ulcer kept him in Italy.

~

Known as a great preacher, he worked for the devotion to the Sacred Heart, Immaculate Conception, and the Way of the Cross, establishing the latter in over five hundred locations.

Once when Leonard was preaching a mission, he noticed some women in the congregation who were rather scantily dressed. In his homily that evening, he advised that all people should be modest in their attire when they come to the Lord's house and left it at that. Unfortunately, the next evening at Mass, these same ladies were still similarly attired. Leonard, not the type of person to shy away from such a challenge, continued his service but, this evening, asked for a special extra contribution with the offering for those "certain poor ladies of the parish who have come to the Mass this evening in spite of the fact that they didn't have enough money to cover their poor, cold bodies."

On being too merciful to sinners, Leonard said: "If the Lord at the moment of my death reproves me for being too kind to sinners, I will answer, 'My dear Jesus, if it is a fault to be too kind to sinners, it is a fault I learned from you, for you never scolded anyone who came to you seeking mercy.'"

NOVEMBER 28
Catherine Labouré
(d. 1876)

A NATIVE OF A SMALL TOWN outside Dijon (France), she was baptized Zoë, the daughter of a farmer. As a result of her mother's death when she was eight, she took over all household duties. For a few years, she also worked in her uncle's café in Paris. Because she had to spend most of her young life in menial service, she was the sole member of her family not to learn to read or write.

~

From the age of fourteen, she felt the calling to follow her elder sister into the religious life. It took some time, but she eventually overcame her father's objections and joined the Sisters of Charity of Saint Vincent de Paul at the age of twenty-four. Once transferred to a convent in Paris, she began to receive prophetic visions of Our Lady.

In the first vision, she was awakened by a "shining child" who led her to the chapel where Our Lady appeared and told her she would have to undertake a difficult task. In the second and third visions, Mary appeared in the same chapel in the form of a picture, standing on a globe, with shafts of light coming from her hands. She was surrounded with the words: "O Mary, conceived without sin, pray for us who have recourse to thee!" The picture turned and on the reverse there appeared a capital letter "M" with a cross above it and two hearts: one crowned with thorns, one pierced with a sword beneath it. Catherine heard a voice telling her to have a medal made, promising that all who would wear it would receive great graces. Similar visions appeared to her for a number of months.

Catherine confided her visions and their contents to her confessor who persuaded the archbishop to have the medal made. In June 1832, the first few thousand were made—many millions would subsequently follow—of the medal now known as the Miraculous Medal. Inquiries were made regarding the authenticity of her visions, but Catherine begged that her identity be kept a secret, and it was. The visions were subsequently judged to be authentic.

Catherine quietly retired to a convent outside Paris to live out the remainder of her earthly life.

Catherine said: "I knew nothing, I was nothing. For this reason, God picked me out."

It is to the Miraculous Medal that the famous conversion, in 1842, of Alphonse Ratisbonne is attributed. He was an Alsatian Jew who, having been persuaded to wear the medal, received a vision of Our Lady, became a priest, and founded the religious congregation known as the Fathers and Sisters of Zion.

Fittingly, when Catherine's mother died when she was eight years old, she went back to her room after the funeral, took Our Lady's statue from the wall, addressed it, and said: "Now, dear Lady, you are to be my mother."

December

~

DECEMBER 1
Eligius of Noyon
(d. 660)

APPRENTICED AS A GOLDSMITH to the master of the mint at Limoges, Eligius is one of the Fourteen Holy Helpers. He came to the attention of King Clotaire II who made him an officer of his treasury. Soon Eligius's great talent for working in precious metals made him a person of rank and wealth. Though Eligius wore the silk robes of the court, he was uncorrupted by luxury and his wealth was devoted to the poor.

After Clotaire's death, Eligius was appointed counselor to his son, King Dagobert. When Dagobert gave Eligius land at Solignac, he founded a monastery there, as well as setting up the first ever workshop for producing Limoges enamels. Eligius also used his wealth to convert a house in Paris into a convent for women.

~

Eligius was ordained in 640 and he was named bishop of Noyon, spreading the Gospel throughout his large diocese for nineteen years. Eligius foresaw his own death and, falling ill, he called together his household. As death approached, Eligius said to his flock, "Do not weep. Congratulate me instead. I have waited a long time for this release."

Eligius's association with horses came about through this story: A horse that Eligius had been riding was inherited by a priest, but the new bishop liked the horse and took it for himself. The horse became ill as soon as he was stabled under the bishop's roof and nothing could cure him. Meanwhile the priest prayed for the horse's return. The bishop gave back the useless horse, and the animal promptly recovered, a cure attributed to Eligius. Since that time, in some places, horses are blessed on his feast day.

Eligius was ordered by King Clotaire to make him a chair of state, decorated with gold and precious stones. With the materials given to him, Eligius made two chairs, impressing the king to such an extent with his honesty that he made him master of the mint.

Once a stranger asked the way to Eligius's home in Paris and was told to go to a certain street where he would recognize the house by the great confluence of poor people waiting outside.

Eligius received an additional piece of land for a construction project. When he found he had gone over its boundary, he went to the king to apologize. Dagobert said: "Some of my officers do not scruple to rob me of whole estates; whereas Eligius is afraid of having one inch of ground which is not his."

One sermon attributed to Eligius warns against superstitious practices: "Do not trust those who put their faith in magical practices, in fortunetellers, sorcerers, in wizards: do not seek from them help for any cause or infirmity: do not consult them for anything."

John Ruysbroeck

(d. 1381)

BORN NEAR BRUSSELS, John founded a monastery after his ordination. Here he wrote many spiritual works, which have given rise to his reputation as a prominent medieval mystic.

∽

Here is John's explanation of love: "Those who follow the way of love are the richest of all men living: They are bold, frank, and fearless. They have neither travail nor care, for the Holy Ghost bears all their burdens. They do not affect singular conduct. They are just like other good men."

John says this about the fruitfulness of grace: "But although, even as God is common to all, the sun shines upon all trees, yet many a tree remains without fruits, and many a tree brings forth wild fruits of little use to men. And for this reason such trees are pruned, and shoots of fruitful trees are grafted into them, so that they may bear good fruits, savory and useful to man. The light of Divine grace is a fruit-bearing shoot, coming forth from the living paradise of the eternal kingdom; and no deed can bring refreshment or profit to man if it be not born of this shoot. This shoot of Divine grace, which makes man pleasing to God, and through which he merits eternal life, is offered to all men. But it is not grafted into all, because some will not cut away the wild branches of their trees; that is, unbelief, and a perverse and disobedient will opposed to the commandments of God."

John makes this observation: "One person works upon another person from the outside inwards, but God alone comes to us from within outwards."

Francis Xavier

(d. 1552)

PATRON OF THE FOREIGN MISSIONS *and colleague of Saint Ignatius Loyola, Francis Xavier was born in the family's castle in Navarre. He was ordered by Ignatius to journey to the Far East, visiting India, Ceylon, Malaya, Japan, and other places. He left on his mission within twenty-four hours of receiving Ignatius's command, pausing only long enough to patch an old pair of trousers. His mission met with great difficulties but Francis Xavier's talents and determination overcame them. In a letter to Ignatius, Francis wrote: "My arms are often almost paralyzed with baptizing and my voice gives out completely through endlessly repeating the creed, the commandments, the prayers, and a sermon on heaven and hell." Francis died near Hong Kong when he was about to enter China to open up another land for Christ.*

~

About missionary travel, Francis said: "There is no better rest in this restless world than to face imminent peril of death solely for the love and service of God," and "Do not fix your residence in any one spot, but go round all the time from village to village visiting each and every one of the Christians, as I did when I was there."

About treating people mercifully: "I entreat you to bear yourself very lovingly towards those people...for if they love you and get on well with you, you will do great service to God. Learn to pardon and support their weaknesses very patiently, reflecting that if they are not so good now, they will be some day."

John Damascene

(d. *c.*749)

MONK, THEOLOGIAN, DOCTOR OF THE CHURCH, John served as a representative of Christians at the court of the caliph. He then undertook the monastic life, boldly opposing iconoclastic forces. He authored the first real compendium of theology, the Fountain of Wisdom, *saying "I shall add nothing of my own, but shall gather together into one those things which have been worked out by the most eminent of teachers."*

John writes that maintaining Church tradition fosters virtue: "Order is good; the breakdown of order is evil…the natural order is obedience to the Creator: disobedience is chaos…We must submit humbly to God as our creator, and conform to the creator's laws."

John's summary of the eight evils: "The thoughts that encompass all evil are eight in number: those of gluttony, unchastity, avarice, anger, dejection, listlessness, self-esteem, and pride. It does not lie within our power to decide whether or not these eight thoughts are going to arise and disturb us. But to dwell on them or not to dwell on them, to excite the passions or not to excite them, does lie within our power."

Ambrose

(d. 397)

A ROMAN NOBLE, Ambrose was educated in the classics. A famous orator and governor of Milan, he converted to Christianity. Ordained in 374, he was a writer and, as well, it was he who worked to convert Saint Augustine of Hippo (he baptized him). He was proclaimed a Doctor of the Church by Pope Boniface VIII in 1298. The title the "Honey-tongued Doctor" was given to him (because he was such a great speaker) and led to the use of bees and all that is associated with them in images representing Ambrose.

~

Ambrose wrote the following about the attitude of Saint Agnes as she was condemned to be beheaded: "She was filled with happiness at this sentence and went to the gallows more cheerfully than others go to their wedding."

About riches, Ambrose advises: "Riches are the beginning of all vices, because they make us capable of carrying out even our most vicious desires," and "To renounce riches is the beginning and sustaining of virtues."

On revenge, Ambrose gives this advice: "No one can heal himself by wounding someone else."

Assessing the damage wrought by individual bad deeds: "Our own personal bad thoughts and deeds are far more dangerous to us than any enemy from the world."

On reading, Ambrose said "The person who reads a great deal, fills himself up and, when he is full, he can tell others, giving them a taste for it."

On verbal battles: "If you find yourself in the company of people who say wrong things, want a verbal battle, are spiteful, or are most difficult, the wisest thing to do is to remain silent, for what they are seeking from us is a contemptuous reply, or a sarcastic comment. Our silence causes them great difficulty, say nothing, let them stew and "chew the cud of their anger." They have no defense against it and this will easily show them that we do not approve of them or their ways.

DECEMBER 9
Peter Fourier
(d. 1640)

A FRENCH AUGUSTINE PRIEST, ordained in 1589, he was the founder of the religious order known as the Daughters of Our Lady whose mission is to educate girls. In 1597, he was named the parish priest of a particularly sinful district. Through his hard work and prayers, Peter soon restored order. A man also interested in his parishioners' temporal needs, he established a "mutual help" bank called "Saint Evre's Purse" in which money was supplied on a short-loan basis to parishioners in financial difficulty. Peter was exiled for political reasons and spent the years before his death as a teacher in a school which he founded.

~

Since his schools were open to both Catholic and Protestant girls, Peter gave the following instructions to his teachers about how to handle the latter: "Treat them kindly and lovingly….Do not let the children tease them….Do not speak in a derogatory way about their religion, but when a good time comes (of course when speaking generally to your other children), show them how good our religion is."

Peter was never subservient to royalty. A colleague over-head him in a conversation with a duke:

"Your Highness will not do that," said Peter.

"Yes, I shall do it. Why? Who will prevent me?" responded the duke.

"I," said Peter, "for it is not the will of God, and I forbid it."

DECEMBER 11

Damasus I

(pope) (d. 384)

STYLED BY SAINT JEROME as an "incomparable man," Damasus was elected pope in 366 alongside the anti-Pope, Ursinus: both served simultaneously. Damasus was a writer and he is reported to have been the person who commissioned Jerome to make the translation of the Scriptures we now know as the Vulgate. A great restorer of catacombs, shrines, and tombs, he is considered the patron of archeologists for this reason. He died at the age of eighty, writing his general epitaph for the papal burial spot in the cemetery of Saint Callistus in this way: "I, Damasus, wish to be buried here, but I feared to offend the ashes of these holy ones."

~

As part if his epitaph, Damasus said: "Christ who walking on the sea could calm the bitter waves, who gives life to the dying seeds of the earth; he who was able to loose the mortal chains of death, and after three days' darkness could bring again to the upper world the brother of his sister Martha: he, I believe, will make Damasus rise again from the dust."

Jane Frances de Chantal
(d. 1641)

DESCRIBED BY SAINT VINCENT DE PAUL as "one of the holiest souls I have ever met," Jane married the Baron de Chantal and spent eight happy years with him before he died in a hunting accident. After his death, Jane took a vow of chastity and raised her four children. She found her spiritual father in Saint Francis de Sales and he encouraged her to found the new Order of the Visitation for widows and other women who could not endure the excessive austerities of older orders. On her way home from a visit of charity, Jane fell ill and died soon after.

~

While living at home, Jane followed a strict daily rule. Her household felt the effect of this spiritual path, saying "Madame always prays, yet she is never troublesome to anyone."

About vocations, Jane observed: "Nothing so prevents us from perfecting ourselves in the vocation we have as wishing for another."

Antony Grassi
(d. 1671)

IN SPITE OF FERVENT OPPOSITION from his widowed mother, Antony entered the Oratorian Fathers at the age of seventeen. An excellent student, he had the reputation of being a "walking dictionary." Later, it was said of him that no one ever saw him angry, or even upset. Soon elected superior, a position he would hold for the rest of his life, he was said to have possessed the gift of being able to read people's consciences, not just in general things, but in very specific areas where he would have had no prior knowledge.

A fervent non-believer in physical austerities, he is quoted as having said: "Humbling the mind and will is more effective than a hair shirt between the skin and your clothes."

A great believer in silence and respect for others and using a lowered tone of the voice, he would often say: "Father, give me just a few inches of your voice."

Antony's method of judging a person's character is this: "You cannot judge a person from just one single action or trait, but you must consider the whole. When you look at the whole, you will generally find that the good outweighs the bad."

DECEMBER 14
John of the Cross
(d. 1591)

BORN INTO POVERTY, John became a Carmelite at the age of twenty-one and was ordained a priest at the age of twenty-five. He decided to live a life that was more severe than the one he was living and, at the urging of Teresa of Ávila, he instituted the primitive reform within the order and took the name John of the Cross. Not well accepted by some of his brothers, he was imprisoned, but escaped after nine months, although his reforms revitalized the Carmelites. A great spiritual writer and mystic, John was made a Doctor of the Church in 1926.

~

John said of Christ's disciples: "The soul of a person who is a servant of God is full of joy...and is always ready to burst into song."

Teresa of Ávila was anxious to have John's order (the discalced or barefoot friars) become the confessors for her convent, but many of the religious there felt that the discalced friars were too severe and opposed her on this matter. So, whenever a religious sister would go into a confessional, the first thing she would say was: "Are you discalced?" John would pause, look at his bare feet, pull his habit over them, and reply "calced." In time, the religious sisters were pleased to have this "calced" confessor among them.

On union with God, John said: "There is no better or more necessary work than love....We have been created for love....Everything is ordered on the basis of our union in love with God."

On the beauty of nature: "Natural things are always beautiful....For they are the crumbs that fall from God's table."

Here is John's advice on meeting adversity: "Whenever anything disagreeable happens, remember Christ was crucified and be quiet."

About people who complain: "The person who complains is neither perfect, nor a good Christian."

DECEMBER 15
Mary di Rosa
(d. 1855)

MARY LEFT SCHOOL *at seventeen and decided not to marry, giving all of her energies to work with the poor and the sick. An excellent organizer with a good business mind, Mary founded a religious community to look after the sick in hospitals. Its aim was to look after the whole person, not simply to treat an isolated illness. During a period of armed conflict in Italy, Mary set up a military hospital. In the spirit of Florence Nightingale, Mary's congregation had to face the distrust of doctors who were not used to working with women and who thought they were incapable. Won over, the doctors soon accepted the Handmaids of Charity in hospitals and on the battlefield. In 1850, Mary's congregation was approved by Rome, and by 1855 a victim of complete physical exhaustion, she died at Brescia.*

⁓

Always willing to be of service to others, Mary once said: "I can't go to bed with a quiet conscience if during the day I missed any chance, however slight, of preventing wrong doing or of helping to do some good."

DECEMBER 16
Mary of the Angels
(d. 1717)

BORN NEAR TURIN, ITALY, *Mary entered the Carmel of Saint Christina at the age of sixteen. After overcoming a severe bout of homesickness and an intense dislike of her novice mistress, Mary persevered and was professed. After a "dark night of the soul," she began to attain mystical union with God, all the while practicing physical penances such as pressing her tongue with an iron ring and pouring melted wax on her skin. Eventually, Mary was appointed novice mistress herself and three years later prioress. For the last twenty years of her life, she continued to experience mystical gifts.*

~

When Mary was very ill just prior to her death, her nuns asked that she be "given an obedience" to recover. May said: "Obedience wills what God wills, and therefore I will what obedience wills. Were the impossible possible I would do as you ask; but I have so stormed the heart of Jesus to get my desire [to die] that he has granted it."

DECEMBER 17

Olympias
(d. 408)

OLYMPIAS, OFTEN CALLED THE "GLORY" of the widows of the Eastern Church," was widowed shortly after her own marriage. Wishing to dedicate herself to God, she formed a community of virgins in her home under the influence of John Chrysostom. On account of her friendship with him Olympias was exiled and her community dispersed.

~

Olympias was sometimes too generous, too caring ("a precious vase filled with the Holy Spirit") and was told that she should "moderate her generosity so she would not encourage the laziness of those who live off her without needing to...for it is like throwing money into the sea."

DECEMBER 18
Samthann of Clonbroney
(d. 739)

AN IRISH NUN who founded the Clonbroney Abbey in County Longford (Ireland), she was the daughter of an Irish king. Legend says that a miracle prevented her arranged marriage from taking place, after which she became a nun. Very little is known about the remainder of her life.

~

Recorded in her life is the following wise advice: When asked in what position one should pray, she replied: every position—standing, sitting, laying, any way, at all times. When a monk informed her that he was going to stop studying so he could pray more, she told him: "You will never be able to settle your mind and pray if you neglect your studies," and he couldn't. When another monk announced he was making a pilgrimage, she made this remark: "The kingdom of heaven can be reached without crossing any sea, for God is close to all who call out to him."

DECEMBER 19
Urban V
(pope) (d. 1370)

WILLIAM DE GRIMOARD WAS BORN into a well-to-do family. He had a distinguished academic career, studying both the classics as well as teaching canon law at four universities. Joining the Benedictines, he undertook a series of appointments as abbot, diplomat, and canon lawyer.

Elected pope upon the death of Innocent VI in 1362, he was not even a cardinal. Immediately his reforms began. Thousands of scholarships were created, new universities founded. Churches and monasteries that had fallen into disrepair were rebuilt. In 1366, after fifty years in Avignon, Urban wanted to bring the papacy back to Rome. Once in Rome, he wept at the sight of the ruin of the great churches (the Lateran, Saint Peter's and Saint Paul's) and began restoring the city, shaping up the clergy, and reviving religion.

In spite of all his simple but fruitless efforts, he, and the papacy, sadly left Rome and returned to Avignon in 1370 even though Saint Bridget had predicted that he would die an early death if he did so. Urban died just four months later.

~

Knowing his death to be near, Urban had his fellow brothers move him to his brother's home at the foot of the hill. He said that he did not want to die while laying on fine sheets.

It was said of Pope Urban V that his goodness had one defect, he didn't hide it under his hat.

When he agreed to take on his new mission as pope he did so as he always did, without any ceremony, "I pray as everyone prays, I eat as you do….I will also die as you." He also chose the name of Urban because "all the popes called Urban have been saints."

DECEMBER 20

Peter Canisius

(d. 1597)

An outstanding student, Peter had a masters degree by the age of nineteen. His original intention was to become a lawyer, but the secular life did not appeal to him. Taking a vow of celibacy and pursuing his love of theology, he went to Germany and joined the Jesuits. Ordained in 1564, he became a sought-after preacher.

As a delegate to the Council of Trent, Ignatius of Loyola asked Peter to go to Rome to help him for five months. Peter then set about reforming schools and universities in Germany, as well as successfully preaching for conversions. He was called to Vienna by the King to do the same there. Finding the situation disgraceful—churches in ruin, monasteries deserted, no ordinations for twenty years, he set to work. Also, during this time he wrote what is considered his finest work, the Summary of Christian Doctrine. *Moving to Prague in 1556, Peter founded a college which gained such a reputation that even the Protestants sent their children to it. Moving back to Germany at the King's request, he convinced the government to restore public schools. Throughout his life he insisted on the importance of schools and writing for publication.*

~

Peter's approach to responding to Protestant criticism was to respond to it in an intelligent way. When his opponents were right, he told them so. He felt he could win any Christian debate, preferring to concentrate on doctrine rather than controversy. He always assumed that Protestants erred out of ignorance rather than malice.

Here is Peter's focus on disaster: "Let the world indulge its own kind of madness....It will not last very much longer, it will die away as quickly as a shadow. Buried deep in Christ's wounds, why should we worry?"

On time management: "If you have a great deal to do, God will help you to find the time to do it all."

On salvation: "You [Christ] promised me a garment that was made of three things to cover the nakedness of my soul: peace, love, and perseverance. Protected by this garment of salvation, I am confident that I will need nothing else, will be successful in everything I do, and give you great glory."

DECEMBER 22
Frances Xavier Cabrini
(d. 1917)

ONE OF THIRTEEN CHILDREN of an Italian farmer, she received a convent education and training as a teacher. She tried to join a religious order at the age of eighteen, but could not because of her poor health. Asked to teach at a girl's school, the House of Providence Orphanage, she did so for six years. Finally, she was able to take her religious vows in 1877. She was so devoted to her work that in 1880, when the orphanage closed, her bishop asked her to found the Order of the Missionary Sisters of the Sacred Heart of Jesus. Its focus would be to care for the poor children in schools and hospitals. Pope Leo XIII sent her to the United States to carry on this mission.

Mother Cabrini and six of her sisters arrived in New York in 1889 to do their work among immigrants, especially the Italians. In all, she founded sixty-seven institutions—schools, hospitals, and orphanages in the United States, Italy, and South America. Mother Cabrini, like many of those who worked with her became a United States citizen.

~

Mother Cabrini developed the habit of strolling along Wall Street, stopping at whatever office she felt might be sympathetic to her cause (although she gave the air of not having any particular motive for these visits).

On one of her strolls, Mother Cabrini stopped and knocked at the door of a successful business and asked to see the company president, of course, without an appointment. His secretary asked Mother to be seated and slipped into her boss's office, asking him what he wanted to do. He angrily replied: "I guess I'll have to see her. The sooner I see her, the sooner she'll leave us alone. Show her in, but come in after five minutes and tell me that there is pressing business that awaits me."

Mother Cabrini was shown into the president's office with the admonition that he was very busy, only taking time to see her because his secretary insisted.

Mother Cabrini replied: "I fully understand. I also abhor wasting time. I have come to ask…"

The president interrupted her: "…for money?"

"No, not for money, for your advice. I know that you are an astute businessman. I trust you and have faith in you. Your advice is worth more to me than money," replied Mother Cabrini.

She continued on and explained that she needed his "expert" advice to find the needed capital to finance the building of a "small" home for one hundred or so orphans. The president suddenly remembered a building he owned that wasn't being used, yet he continued to listen to Mother speak, just to see if her plans were realistic.

Five minutes came and went, the secretary came in. The company president told her to leave them and to hold all of his calls.

Mother Cabrini then continued: "I know of this place

on the banks of the wonderful Hudson River where my children could play, take in good fresh air and grow strong. And...the price is not high."

Needless to say, Mother Cabrini was speaking of the very same unused building that the president owned. How could this powerful businessman resist? Performing a good deed, he gave Mother Cabrini the building.

DECEMBER 23
John of Kanty
(d. 1473)

A BRILLIANT STUDENT at the University of Krakow and later a priest and professor of theology at that same university, John was removed from his position due to false accusations planted by rivals and assigned to parish work in Bohemia. Several years later, he returned to Krakow and taught Scripture for the remainder of his life.

~

A serious, humble man, generous with the poor, he slept very little, ate sparsely, especially no meat. He went on pilgrimage to Jerusalem on at least four occasions. He was warned to care for his health, but his reply was that the early Church Fathers had lived in far worse conditions.

John was a humble priest, depriving himself of the luxury of wearing new clothing. As was the custom, he was often invited to dine with the nobles of his parish. One evening, accepting such an invitation, he presented himself at the door of one such nobleman but was refused entrance by his doorman because of his tattered cassock. Father John returned home and proceeded to change into a new one he had just received but had put into storage. Returning to the nobleman's home soon after and now gaining entrance, he was served a wonderful meal, but the occasion was spoiled when a servant spilled a tray of food on the priest, staining his new garb. Calming the man, John turned to him and said: "Don't be concerned, my cassock deserves some supper, too, for if it hadn't been for this new cassock, I would not be here."

A story is told that once, when John was dining, a beggar passed. John jumped up and carried his full plate to feed him, looking for others. When he returned to continue his meal, his very same plate was on the table, full of food.

John's advice to his students: "fight all false opinions, let your arms be patience, love, and sweetness of manner. If you are tough, it is bad for your soul and ruins even the best arguments."

DECEMBER 26
Vincentia Lopez y Vicuna
(d. 1896)

THE DAUGHTER OF A SPANISH LAWYER, she was sent to Madrid to live with an aunt while she was in school. She was so strong-willed that she refused to marry the man her parents had chosen because she wanted to follow her aunt's example of religious devotion. After much persuasion, they finally relented and allow her to become a religious when she was nineteen.

Along with her aunt, she formed a group of organized, devoted women who would take care of women in domestic service. In 1878, they founded the Daughters of Mary Immaculate for Domestic Service. Vincentia and three others pronounced their vows at that time. This congregation soon spread throughout Europe and Latin America.

Here is Vincentia's explanation of her vocation: "The dedication of one's life in service to their fellow man reflects the level of devotion and care that Mary and Joseph showed in Bethlehem. Reaching out to others permits us to do the work of the Lord."

Vincentia's advice to her sisters: "Love one another in God and for God, and see God himself in your Sisters, as the Rule tells us; fix your eyes on their qualities, and not on their faults, unless it be for the sake of compassion and of mutual help in counseling them."

DECEMBER 28
Gaspar del Bufalo
(d. 1837)

GASPAR WAS DEDICATED by his mother to religious service at the age of eighteen months after prayers to Saint Francis Xavier cured him of a severe eye disease. He became a Jesuit and was ordained in 1808. In Rome, Gaspar founded the congregation of the Missioners of the Precious Blood, devoted to preaching and parish missions. Gaspar's preaching was said to have been "like a spiritual earthquake." He is especially renowned for his conversion of the mountain guerillas who would come from their mountain hideouts, lay their guns down, and convert. Gaspar was targeted by the anger of those who profited from the guerillas's depredations, and these people were able to convince Pope Leo XII to suspend Gaspar's efforts, but after a personal audience, the pope was heard to comment: "Del Bufalo is an angel." In 1834, he founded the women's congregation that is devoted to providing education for girls.

In his refusal to take an oath of allegiance to Napoleon, Gaspar uttered these famous words: "*Non posso, non debbo, non voglio*" which mean I cannot; I ought not; I will not."

Gaspar said: "Missionaries must be ready for anything, and like soldiers and sailors, they must never surrender."

DECMBER 29
Thomas à Becket
(d. 1170)

ARCHBISHOP OF CANTERBURY, killed in his cathedral by four of King Henry II's men, Thomas is the most famous martyr of the Middle Ages. During most of his life, Thomas was worldly and impetuous, but his consecration changed his way of life from "a follower of hounds to a shepherd of souls."

～

About the continuity of the Church, Thomas said: "Many are needed to plant and water what has been planted now that the faith has spread so far and there are so many people....No matter who plants or waters, God gives no harvest unless what is planted is the faith of Peter and unless he agrees to his teachings."

About winning the race for salvation, Thomas remarks: "Remember the sufferings of Christ, the storms that were weathered...the crown that came from those sufferings which gave new radiance to the faith....All saints give testimony to the truth that without real effort, no one ever wins the crown."

Thomas requested this favor of his friend Herbert of Bosham on his way to his ordination: "Hereafter, I want you to tell me, candidly and in secret, what people are saying about me. And if you see anything in me that you regard as a fault, feel free to tell me in private. For from now on, people will talk about me, but not to me. It is dangerous for men in power if no one dares to tell them when they go wrong."

INDEX

〜

Peter Gonazlez 65
Peter of Alexandria 215
Peter of Alcántara 195
Peter of Luxemburg 115
Petroc 98
Philip Neri 91
Philip of Zell 79
Philip Powell 113
Pius X (pope) 146
Pius V (pope) 76
Poemen 152
Porphyry 36
Procopius 117

R

Raymond of Pennafort 6
Richard Gwyn 194
Richard Thirkeld 94
Richarius 72
Rita of Cascia 89
Romuald 106
Rose of Lima 148
Rupert of Salzburg 55

S

Salaun 201
Samthann of Clonbroney 232
Schetzelon 136
Scholastica 29
Sisoes 116
Sozon 162
Stephen I (pope) 132
Sulpicius Severus 21

T

Teilo 28
Teresa of Ávila 190
Theodore of Sykeon 70
Theodosius 119
Thérèse of Lisieux 178
Thomas More 108
Thomas à Becket 240
Thomas of Villanova 170
Thomas Aquinas 20

U

Urban V (pope) 232

V

Veronica Giuliani 118
Vincent de Paul 174
Vincent Pallotti 14
Vincent Ferrer 61
Vincentia Lopez y Vicuna 238

W

Willibrord of Utrrecht 205
Wulfstan of Worcester 13

Z

Zita 73